ONE FLEW OVER THE ONION DOME

St Vladimir's Seminary Press

ORTHODOXY AND MISSIONS SERIES

Number 2

Missiology is one of the newest disciplines now accepted in the academy. This series presents historical and contemporary perspectives on the theology of mission, evangelism, church growth, new church planting, parish revitalization, catechetical material for adult converts, and comparative religion. Challenges and opportunities—both domestic and foreign—in the field of missiology will form the core of this series.

Chad Hatfield
Series Editor

One Flew over the Onion Dome

*American Orthodox Converts,
Retreads, & Reverts*

FR JOSEPH HUNEYCUTT

ST VLADIMIR'S SEMINARY PRESS
YONKERS, NY 10707
2018

Library of Congress Cataloging-in-Publication Data

Names: Huneycutt, Joseph David, author.
Title: One flew over the onion dome : American orthodox converts, retreads, and
    reverts / by Fr. Joseph David Huneycutt.
Description: Yonkers, NY : St Vladimir's Seminary Press, 2018. | Series: Orthodoxy
    and missions series, number 2 | Originally published: Salisbury, Mass. : Regina
    Orthodox Press, c2006. | Includes bibliographical references.
Identifiers: LCCN 2017057733 (print) | LCCN 2017058747 (ebook) | ISBN
    9780881416169 | ISBN 9780881416152 (alk. paper)
Subjects: LCSH: Orthodox Eastern converts—United States.
Classification: LCC BX739.A1 (ebook) | LCC BX739.A1 H86 2018 (print) |
    DDC 281.9/73—ds23
LC record available at https://lccn.loc.gov/ 2017057733

COPYRIGHT © 2018
ST VLADIMIR'S SEMINARY PRESS
575 Scarsdale Rd, Yonkers, NY 10707
1–800–204–2665
www.svspress.com

ISBN 978–0-88141–615–2 (paper)
ISBN 978–0-88141–616–9 (electronic)

PRINTED IN THE UNITED STATES OF AMERICA

For my dad, Malcolm

(1941–2005)

Memory Eternal!

———————————

"The Convert experience is full of surprises, not only for the pilgrims involved but for those who attempt to pastor and teach them. *One Flew Over the Onion Dome* tackles these challenges with up-front honesty, good humor, and steadfast faith."

Frederica Mathewes-Green, NPR commentator and author

"In recent years Orthodox churches in America have received a multitude of Converts from a variety of different backgrounds. Many books have been published to tell the story of individual and group conversions. In the pages of *One Flew Over the Onion Dome* the reader will find a reasoned explanation, formed through both personal experience and observation, that tells not only stories but provides a much needed guide for the clergy called to form and pastor these various Converts."

The Very Rev. Dr Chad Hatfield, President,
St Vladimir's Orthodox Theological Seminary

"Fr Joseph Huneycutt's book is reminiscent of John Bunyan's *Pilgrim's Progress*, in that it details the pitfalls, traps, and snares that so easily entrap those who set out to travel the narrow Way. Likewise, he points out the underlying spiritual maladies of the soul and how to avoid the various pitfalls. Many may be able to point out the problems and encounters, even giving them a name. But to identify a problem, i.e., a spiritual malady, is not the same thing as being able to cure it. Overcoming the problem is a different matter entirely. Thanks be to God he offers helpful pastoral counsel to those who must travel and guide others in this difficult path we are called to travel."

+MARK, Archbishop of Eastern Pennsylvania (OCA)

"We have found the Pearl of Great Price, could be a subtitle to this gem, *One Flew Over the Onion Dome*. It is a precious collection of heart-beats reflecting the various facets of the same pilgrimage that St Paul made when called by Christ on the road to Damascus: scrutiny and doubt from Cradles, heart-wrenching rejection by family and friends, periodic re-consideration while zealously bearing fruit in the Lord, delight in the "coming home," humble acknowledgement of the gift received. "My story is not much different from the host of other stories of Americans converting to Eastern Orthodox Christianity," confesses Fr Joseph Huneycutt. Although each story has a thread common to the others, each one is singular because it is the life-searching quest of a unique soul longing "in the present age," for "the knowledge of the truth and in the future age, everlasting life.

This is a must read for Cradles who might need to re-appreciate the Truth, for Seekers who have found the way but must patiently walk it while waiting for what blessed life which is to come and especially for hierarch under whose omophorions the Good Shepherd has led these sheep for pastoring and who will be called to account for their eternal well-being."

+NATHANIEL, Archbishop of Detroit (OCA)

"This book is like a map for the new Convert, which shows where the pits and the dead ends are, and most importantly, how to find the treasure. For clergy, it will be a helpful tool in diagnosing common convert ailments before they become spiritually terminal."

Fr John Whiteford, author of Sola Scriptura *and a priest of the Russian Orthodox Church Abroad*

Table of Contents

Acknowledgements

*O*ne *Flew Over the Onion Dome* began as a presentation for clergy entitled "American Converts and the Pastoral Issues They Bring to the Church." I am indebted to Archpriest David Moser of St Seraphim Church, Boise, Idaho, for inviting me to speak on the subject at the Cathedral of the Mother of God—Joy of All Who Sorrow, San Francisco, in the spring of 2002.

I must also express my deep and humble appreciation to Metropolitan PHILIP, of thrice blessed memory, His Eminence, Metropolitan JOSEPH, His Grace, Bishop BASIL, and all Orthodox Hierarchs who not only welcome American converts into their "families" under their Domes but paternally tolerate our tics, tantrums, and often misguided zeal.

I owe a tremendous debt of gratitude to the parishioners who have tolerated my many mistakes over the years; they are wonderful teachers. May God grant them good health, long life, and many years!

All examples and stories within the book, except Larry Nevell's are based on real people and actual events. I have tried, perhaps poorly, to mask identities and prevent embarrassment. If my words offend, I beg your forgiveness.

Introduction

1

The Handicapped Convert

L arry Nevell was driving pretty well for a blind man. "Frrrrrrrp," meant he was too close to danger on his right. "Fudup, fudup, fudup," meant he was straddling the center line. Silence indicated smooth sailing.

He'd had trouble finding the car without drawing attention. The "Bwwap, bwwap, bwwap," from the third button in the middle of the key's remote seemed loud and incessant. The car was over to his left, down about 20 fenders. As planned, he'd left his cane and eye wear in his briefcase and pulled his ball cap down over his eyes to avoid being noticed. At first he'd worried that finding the vehicle would pose the greatest challenge. It proved to be only the first of many.

Thirteen, fourteen, fifteen . . . he let his right hand brush past each auto. He had to be getting close. Tapping the middle button one more time, "Bwwap," proved sufficient. Thank God for remote keys!

He was shaking as he sat behind the wheel. Blind from birth, he'd had lots of experience sitting behind the steering wheel, playing. It would take the fingers of both hands to recount the car batteries he'd drained to listen to the radio. He knew every announcer, every song. He'd even memorized commercials—over the past 16 years. Now, on his 21st birthday, he was finally going to take the car for a spin. Scared and excited, he wondered how it might end.

His father had parked the car in the final slot at the end of the third row of the K-Mart lot. This he knew for a fact. Daddy always claimed he was getting his exercise with the small walk to the store—and besides, he'd rather let the elderly and lazy have the nearest parking spots.

Having calmed down from his solo journey to the car, he'd cranked the engine and listened to the radio for a long time before releasing the brake and gearing up. Why do they never tell the time anymore? Finally, 2:30 pm. It was early. Would a blind man driving down the interstate draw more attention in the middle of the day? Or would it be best to save his inaugural drive till the middle of the night? He decided to make the trip in stages.

First he drove down to the car wash. It was only one block from his Dad's favorite parking spot. Down the hill, to the left; he drove extremely slowly. If he bumped someone, it would not really matter. Turning left over the small entry road proved no trouble. Besides, from the gentle clicking noise, he knew that he'd engaged the flashing emergency lights.

The entry to the car wash was, as he'd suspected, idiot proof. You'd have thought the designers had the blind in mind during construction: narrow curbing, sensory activated, automated voices, bells, and whistles. His Dad liked a clean car and Larry knew all the sounds by heart. Having activated the machinery with his Dad's code, Larry sat back and enjoyed the whir-ring and whooshing amid the flip, flap, and drizzle.

He thought about how lucky he was. His brother, Tom, had worked on the state road crew during his college years. He was the one who had explained all the noises to Larry: "Frrrrrrrp" was caused by the warning indicators placed near the shoulder of the road; "Fudup" was the reflectors on the center line. Hearing that there were no stop lights on the interstate, Larry began to imagine the day that he would drive. "Humph!" would have been the response if he'd ever told anyone.

"Ding!" As the car wash was ended, Larry was exhausted. Less than thirty minutes into his big tour, he needed some rest. He eased back onto the service road and headed down to the gas station on the right. Thank God no one was in his Dad's favorite diagonal Disability spot. Larry eased the car into park and rested his head on the seat. He would not be able to stay here long. His Dad said there were cameras everywhere these days, especially at convenience stores. Though Larry couldn't see, he under-stood he was being watched.

Bump, bump, bump! "Hey buddy, are you okay?" Waking from slumber, Larry turned his head toward the window. "What?" He hoped he didn't look blind as he spoke. They said that blind people all acted like Stevie Wonder (whatever that meant). "Your flashers are on!" With a wave of his hand and a press of the button, Larry avoided discovery.

How long had he been asleep? "The White House today..." brccccccccct "I've got friends in low places ..." brccccccccct "sale ends Saturday ..." brccccccccct "low tonight in the mid-forties ..." brccccccccct "Bada-r-r-r-ruum ... Bhaa, bhaa, bhaa-bhaa!, from ABC News ..." Ah, the news. It must be the top of the hour, three o'clock.

Larry started the engine, placed it in reverse, then he panicked. He'd never figured on having to back up. He knew how to engage the car, but how do those who can see do this? Should he turn his head to look behind him or use the mirrors? What if someone was behind him? He decided to punt. That is, he got out of the car and made his way inside the convenience store hoping—without his cane, normal dress, and father—to go unrecognized. All alone, he was buying time.

* * *

Similar to Larry Nevell, many converts enter the strange new world of Orthodoxy trying to make it on their own flawed knowledge and relying on the familiar. This can prove to be frustrating. In the story, Larry is destined, by virtue of his limitations, for failure if he continues his journey handicapped and alone. One must admit, a blind man driving a car is preposterous. Then again, an American converting to Eastern Orthodox Christianity is often viewed as equally absurd.

For Americans, the *study* of Christianity can become one's religion. The convert's path is often navigated by this "science" of faith. Like Larry Neville, we've imbibed of the script, songs, and other media of Christianity so long that we've memorized it. Hungering for more, we long for something new. Often, however, this hunger is insatiable due to our fickle faddishness. Thus, our Christian experience can seem as transient as the Top-40 songs of the day. Ever unsure of ourselves, much like Larry's hope of driving down the Interstate blindly, we struggle to be Orthodox all the while not drawing attention to ourselves, to our shortcomings, to our blindness.

Like the carwash, baptism/chrismation is often the easy part. It's driving the car, moving on from there, that proves challenging. The Church provides human assistance in the form of godparents, confessors, and the Fathers and confessors who've made the journey before. Yet our stubborn self-will oftentimes prevents us from fully taking advantage of such chaperones and chauffeurs. Rather, in typical American fashion, we try to go it alone. Larry believes that he knows more than his father. As an adventurous kid might lie to his father in order to take a joy ride, American converts are tempted to flee their priest, confessor, bishop, and parish. Oftentimes, godparents are mere acquaintances or joyride pals.

As with Larry's memorizing his brother's definition of road sounds, we memorize pithy sayings that we believe will prevent us from falling off the path; it's part of our American rugged individualism. Even when help knocks on our door, we oftentimes wave it away, determined to make it on our own.

We're *supposed* to work out our salvation in community—with godparents, priests, and fellow Pilgrims struggling toward the Kingdom. The Church is not a club where we chose our leader, our companions, or even our priest. Struggling to go it alone, thinking we know better, is as dangerous as driving a car without benefit of sight; and it sure isn't Orthodox.

"Blinded by the Light" is a convert's dilemma. Having found the Pearl of Great Price and drunk deeply from the Well; having been washed in the living waters of baptism and tasted the Medicine of Immortality . . . sometimes we are tempted to want *more*! The early stages of our Conversion were so awesome that the day-to-day salvific struggle seems mundane, boring. We discover that we're still addicted to familiar sins. We're the same sinners as before! And, as fallen human nature is wont to tempt us, we look elsewhere for a solution. Some look for someone to blame. Others look for a guru. Others are tempted to find communities far away and with less accountability. Still others are drawn toward more book knowledge and less human interaction. And like Larry Nevell in our story, these temptations buy only *wasted* time.

Oftentimes, especially as Pastors in missions, we tend to place our hopes on every warm body that darkens the door of our church. Time has proven that this tendency can lead to continual discouragement. Yet we must stay the course! Sow seed. Be faithful. God will provide the increase. Fr Alexander Elchaninov writes:

> Our continual mistake is that we do not concentrate upon the present day, the actual hour, of our life; we live in the past or in the future; we are continually expecting the coming of some special moment when our life will unfold itself in its full significance. And we do not notice that life is flowing like water through our fingers, sifting like precious grain from a loosely fastened bag.
>
> Constantly, each day, each hour, God is sending us people, circumstances, tasks, which should mark the beginning of our renewal; yet we pay them no attention, and thus continually we resist God's will for us. Indeed, how can God help us? Only by sending us in our daily life certain people, and certain coincidences of circumstance. If we accepted every hour of our life as the hour of God's will for us, as the decisive, most important, unique hour of our life—what sources of joy, love, strength, as yet hidden from us, would spring from the depths of our soul!
>
> Let us then be serious in our attitude towards each person we meet in our life, towards every opportunity of performing a good deed; be sure that you will then fulfill God's will for you in these very circumstances, on that very day, in that very hour.[1]

Otherwise, as in the introductory story of Larry, it all makes for good fiction. Yet our salvation is based in Reality. We all fall short. We all miss the mark. This does not mean that we are defeated. We are, however, handicapped. We need each other in Christ. It is the very reason for the Church, the Ark of our Salvation. One has to *live* the Orthodox Christian faith. It is not found in books, gurus, or exotic places. Like the Kingdom of God, it is found within the heart. We have to make room! For dragons

---

[1] Alexander Elchaninov, *The Diary of a Russian Priest* (Crestwood, NY: St Vladimir's Seminary Press, 1982), p. 157.

and slithery passions are also found therein, whose goal it is to smother the light with their darkness. It is their goal to blind us. This is spiritual warfare. It begins with you, directed toward God, working out your salvation with your neighbor. It's like driving a car, with all the struggles and temptations the road brings, with eyes open wide.

2

Convert Frustration

I am an American convert to Orthodox Christianity. I was reared a Southern Baptist, became an Episcopalian, and converted to Orthodoxy in 1993. I am the Chief of Sinners and have often joked of the book I should one day write from a convert priest's perspective entitled *Mistakes I've Made*. Then again, that which has often prevented me from writing at all is fear of falling into the category of "those who read two books and write the third." All this is to say that, due to my pride and sinfulness, I am not qualified as an expert on anything save my own baggage and shortcomings. But I did spend twelve years working in the mission field of the South: North Carolina, South Carolina, Tennessee, Georgia, and Virginia. Most of this effort was expended on American converts and in planting new missions. During that time there were joys and sorrows and, in the eyes of the world, failure and success. In spite of my shortcomings, for which I beg your forbearance, I hope to address honestly the pastoral issues that I've witnessed as Americans struggle toward the ancient Christian faith of holy Orthodoxy.

I will assume that when we say "Americans," we are referring to folks born in this country and raised in a non-Orthodox or nominally-Orthodox environment. By "converts," we are referring to Americans who have been received into the Orthodox Church after previously being members of some other Christian organization, recognizing that this exposure to Christianity may be nominal in some and extreme in others. Since virtually all I know is converts, some of what I say may no doubt be universal with "convert" and "cradle" alike.[1] And, being an American convert

[1]Cradle: an informal term describing those who have been Orthodox, baptized, since they were a baby.

myself, all things may (only) pertain to me. Nonetheless, I will be address-
ing American Christian converts to Orthodox Christianity.

There are two other labels that further define American converts:
reverts and retreads. "Reverts" refers to those who were raised in an
Eastern Orthodox Christian home and left the faith, only to later return.
"Retread" is a name for clergy who convert to Orthodoxy after being
ordained previously in another Christian group. All three of these groups
bring their own pastoral issues and personal struggles to the Church. The
result can be humorous, even maddening, hence the title: "One Flew Over
the Onion Dome."

It is not my purpose in this little book to provide answers and remedies
to the questions and maladies that plague American Orthodoxy in the
twenty-first century. However, I would fail in my goals if I did not supply
a few poor suggestions for our common plight. Therefore, the book is
divided into three sections: "My Story," "Your Story," and "Our Story." It's
my hope that there's a little something here for everyone.

*First of all, we must admit that there exists no small amount of American
Orthodox convert frustration.*

"Welcome Home!" These are sweet words to a convert's ears. Many
come home to holy Orthodoxy after a long and painful spiritual fight
within another Christian body. Some Orthodox Christian believers have
not felt welcome *anywhere*—let alone their own church—for quite some
time. And, even though the sweet words of "Welcome Home" ring true to
their ears, many enter the true faith with fear and trepidation. Where to
fit in? What does the future hold?

If it did not happen during their catechumenate,[2] it'll happen sooner
or later. The convert meets a lifelong Orthodox Christian (or "cradle")
who seemingly hasn't a clue as to the Church's doctrinal, moral, or pious
teachings. These anchors—Christian doctrine, morals, piety—may represent the very net that, in the end, caught the convert. If the cradle is
unaware of the net, can he be trusted as a fish?

---

[2]Catechumenate: a period of formal instruction in the Orthodox faith in preparation
for baptism/chrismation.

In catechumen class, the seekers were taught that the Orthodox Church is the fullness of the faith and not a *denomination*. Yet, the Newly Illumined[3] will meet those who are not aware of this distinction. Some Orthodox view themselves as merely Greek, Arab, or Russian Christians. Ethnicity and Orthodoxy can either go hand in hand, or prevent hands from meeting.

Then there's the "ecu-maniacs," who are so interested in creating a "super church" that they are willing to water down the holy Orthodox faith in order to accommodate those outside the Church. For these converts, there is no harm done in sharing one's faith, as long as another's is given equal footing in the Kingdom of God. Sort of like saying, "Oh, yes, Orthodoxy is the same faith as yours—just with sacraments, icons, ritual, and incense."

The convert may enter an Orthodox house with little or no icons on the walls. The convert may dine with Orthodox Christians that interpret "fasting" as a foreign word and giving thanks is reserved for Thanksgiving. The convert may encounter Orthodox Christians who *not only* do not have a home altar or prayer corner, but seem to have no rule of prayer and no intention of confessing their sins. In time, the convert may start to feel like a stranger in his new "home" of Orthodoxy.

Then, there are the retreads: Evangelicals who become Orthodox may concentrate more on sermon prep than on liturgical form. They may preach too long and conduct in depth Bible Studies, while their collection of relics, icons, and the like may be sparse. An outsider may leave thinking he'd just attended a Baptist Church with incense. Convert frustration.

Then there's the varied lot of "catholic converts," Anglicans and Romans. Those who come to Orthodoxy from a High Church background may be captivated with newfound hats and vestments. Some of these retreads —who have often left environments of "smells, bells, and anything goes" or "eat, drink, and see Mary"—may be slow in grasping the evangelical fervor that fuels the Evangelicals (and, traditionally, Orthodoxy). For many retreads, priests' beliefs are symbolized by what he wears. Is this

---

[3]Newly Illumined: those recently received into the Church through baptism/chrismation. The term is usually applied for the first 40 days after reception into the Church.

true in Orthodoxy? Also, some may be so fond of Rite that they try to prevent other expressions of the faith, even its fullness, from seeping into their world.

Cradle clergy may seem to pick and choose from the smorgasbord of tradition. They may alternate between traditional clergy dress and gym shorts; between evangelical and hesychast; between isolationism and ecumenism, between "Thou" and "You," between long vigils and merely the highlights of Orthros. These chameleons are hard to label. Not being able to label someone is frustrating. Convert frustration.

Heretic alert! Some converts have grown so used to finding a heretic under every bush that their "antichrist antennae" get a constant workout in the sea of Orthodoxy. These are the folks that monitor each and every move of their priest, bishop, and fellow parishioners in hopes of finding something awry. These people, feeling themselves to be the Savior, have grown so used to bearing the truth's burden that they forget that they're supposed to bear one another's burden. Convert frustration.

Some retreads stumble across a copy of the *Rudder*[4] and fall in love with the law. His sleeves get longer, as does his dress, beard, fasts, and vigils; sermons become peppered with agenda. Suddenly, he and his flock become the only "true" Orthodox; everyone else is viewed as heretics. This community may end up in a splinter group where the casting of stones is almost considered a virtue. Thanks be to God; the Church is saved—others be damned! Convert frustration.

Converts are easy prey to feelings of religious superiority and elitism. Like the "open-minded" New Agers who end up embracing the Hindu faith, many newly illumined Orthodox Christians seek out the most exotic, bizarre, and so-called "mysterious" facets of the Orthodox faith. Having come home to the true faith, many may begin looking down their noses at family, friends, and others that are not as tradition-bound as they are. These converts may actually see themselves as *essential* to the preservation of the true faith. In trying to exercise their newfound vocation

---

[4] *The Rudder*, or *Pedalion*, is a compilation of the sacred and divine canons of the Holy Catholic and Apostolic Church, last published in English by The Orthodox Christian Education Society, Chicago, 1957.

they set themselves up as judges. This is known as trying to "out-orthodox the Orthodox."

A convert's previous religious experience may have involved defini- tive lines of warring characters who seemingly wore white hats and black hats. It was easy to distinguish between good guys and bad guys. These converts may have become so accomplished at this task of judging that they become befuddled in Orthodoxy. "Hard to judge" is, of course, is a blessing. God alone is Judge. The Church has withstood the assaults of the Enemy for 2,000 years; "Oops, here I come, maybe I'll break it!" "Perhaps this Church, founded by Christ, which is Christ, needs me to fine tune or correct it?"

One thing is not hard to figure out: the Church is no utopia. It is the Kingdom *now* but it is perfect in Christ, not in its individual members. Patriarchs and Sextons alike fail and fall. "Welcome home" means more than "Welcome to the Orthodox Church." It means welcome to our home which is "already but not yet." Let us not forget that this earth is not our home. Heaven awaits those of true faith and worship. In bearing one another's burdens we are called to reprove, to forgive, to love, and to admonish. *But we are not called to judge.* Yes, the Holy Spirit gives discern- ment. Yet, discernment differs from *our* judgment in the same way that God's Love differs from worldly lust.

Someone suggested at a pastor's conference that we needed more yayas or babushkas[5] in our churches in America to help guide us toward godli- ness and piety in church. The attending bishop agreed but added a cau- tionary note: "Just because you're old doesn't mean you're holy." By the same token, just because the priest *sleeps* in his cassock, his head resting on the *Rudder*, doesn't mean he's holy. Just because your rule of prayer is three hours a day does not mean you're holy. Just because you were "born Orthodox" doesn't mean you're holy. Just because you can recite the entire Bible, cover to cover, doesn't mean you're holy. Just because you're a member of the holy Orthodox Church doesn't necessarily mean you're holy—let alone the Judge! In this life, *we are all perpetual converts.*

---

[5] *Yaya* or *Babushka*: "grandmother" in Greek and Russian, respectively.

Why do you see the speck in your brother's eye, but do not notice the log that is in your own eye? Or how can you say to your brother, "Let me take the speck out of your eye," when there is a log in your own eye? You hypocrite, first take the log out of your own eye, and then you will see clearly to take the speck out of your brother's eye (Mt 7.3–5).[6]

The Church is full of sinners. God is glorified in His saints. These two sentences portray the essence of our striving. We must seek to be a holy people, while being ever mindful of our shortcomings. Both convert and cradle alike must be vigilant; for the enemy walks around like a roaring lion. Yet, as a friend once reminded me: "He's a toothless lion. Our Lord has defanged him." Nothing is perfect this side of the grave save Christ our true God who has destroyed death. It is our relationship with Him that will save us.

Life with Christ is a continual conversion. It is in Christ that we are converted from dead to living. It is in Christ that we are converted from sinner to saint. It is in Christ that we con-*vert* frustration. I*t is in Christ that we convert.* And the purpose of this little book is not only to address some of the issues faced by converts, reverts, and retreads, but to hopefully offer a small measure of commiseration and a larger dose of comfort.

[6]Scriptural quotes, unless otherwise indicated, taken from the Revised Standard Version.

My Story

3

Stumbling Toward Truth

All American converts to Orthodox Christianity have a story to tell. Mine may not be much different from yours or your neighbor's. But, for sake of background, here follows a portion of my journey.

I like to tell folks that my relationship with God hasn't changed drastically since the days of my youth, growing up a Southern Baptist; now I just know how to worship him. There's some truth to that; mainly it's my relationship with *me* that Orthodoxy has changed. I understand my relationship with God and Church differently.

My family was very much involved in church life: Sunday School, Sunday Morning Worship, Sunday Evening Worship, Youth Group, Royal Ambassadors, Church Camp, and Softball. (Don't laugh. Softball is a big part of Southern Baptist evangelism.) We lived less than a mile from the church and were always there or could be on a moment's notice. My mother was the last one to leave on Sunday. Even the Preacher went home before we did. My dad, brother, and I would often wait in the car while Mom finished talking to the next-to-the-last person to leave from in front of the church. In a matter of five or six hours, we'd be back for more.

I never fully encountered another form of Christianity until I started dating a Roman Catholic girl in high school. Sure, we had Methodists and Pentecostals all around, but they just seemed more moderate or loopy respectively.

I had heard that the Roman Catholics worshiped Mary. So, when I was in the 8th grade, I voluntarily did a term paper on Mariolatry.[1] This

---

[1] Mariolatry: Giving to Mary the worship *(latria)* that is due to God alone (John A. Hardon, S.J., *Pocket Catholic Dictionary* [New York: Doubleday, 1985]).

required me to do some research in the local library where I happened upon a book containing the documents of Vatican II. I was shocked. The Roman Catholics actually believed in Jesus! In fact very little of the book even mentioned the Blessed Virgin Mary. Those portions lent scant evidence that they worshiped her. I became a bit more "ecumenical" from that time on.

Growing up Baptist gave me a firm grasp of the Bible's contents, the heroes of the Christian faith, and the basics of morality. Yet given my studies outside of church and my experiences in church, I never quite understood why we called it a "worship" service. In my view the agenda was: sing a couple songs, have a long prayer, another song, long prayer, big long speech, more hymns, ending prayer, altar call (but no altar), etc. In my young opinion, a cursory viewing of Cecil B. DeMille classics would reveal this format to be a snoozer when it comes to a God desirous of "worship."

I must also admit my teenaged struggle with hypocrisy. My church was not what I would classify "fundamentalist" but, being Baptist, it did frown on drinking, smoking, and dancing. (Unless you were an usher; I don't know about drinking and dancing but, for some reason, most all of the ushers smoked.) But many Sunday mornings, don't ask me how I know, I found myself in church with some of the same folks who'd been out drinking, smoking, and dancing the night before!

One Sunday while I was helping my Mom keep the nursery downstairs, I heard over the speaker system that all of my friends had gone up to commit themselves to Christ. In other words, they were headed toward baptism. I'd missed out. So it was that my struggle with baptism began. I felt abandoned by my friends who'd all gone up en masse. It focused the spotlight on me. Sometime later, I remember a service where I felt the urge to go up front so strongly, and resisted it in equal measure, that I ended up blacking out and slumping down into my pew.

By the time I got to college, I was pretty much down on Christianity until I met a new friend. He had just converted to the Episcopal Church from being a Southern Baptist. He spent a lot of time praying out of a book; so much so that I dubbed him "Guru." This moniker stuck with him through college.

Around the middle of our freshman year he and I began to talk seriously about religion. I shared all of my teenaged concerns, ideas, and struggles. He invited me to church with him. I was reluctant, but agreed to attend a meeting of the Canterbury Club, the college youth group. I was shocked. It was a church cookout and they had, *gasp*, beer and even ash trays! So I went to the Episcopal Church and, with one "minor" exception, never went back to the Baptist church.

My first experience of liturgical worship was, to my virgin eyes, awesome. I saw a procession, banners, ritual, communion—a short sermon. I was hooked. Though far from becoming a "guru," I'd found a new church home in the Episcopal Church. My parents were just pleased I was going to church at all.

Here's the one exception: Though I had no interest in returning to the Protestantism of my youth, I did realize that it was time for me to be baptized. I thought the right thing to do was to go back to my home church and walk that aisle. When I finally did, the Preacher asked if I wanted to join the church. I said, "No, I want to be baptized." We repeated this dialogue several times until he gave up. He was a family friend and knew I was not coming back to the Baptists. At the age of 20, I was baptized in my home church. I then returned to my church home, St Luke's Episcopal, on the campus of Appalachian State University, Boone, North Carolina.

Six years later I married a Baptist girl, a preacher's kid, in the Episcopal Church. She eventually converted and within a year and a half of marriage we arrived at Nashotah House Seminary[2] where I began studying for the priesthood in the fall of 1989.

There's a story there. In my home diocese, most seminarians go to the University of the South,[3] Sewanee, Tennessee. The bishop required me to

[2] Nashotah House, Nashotah, Wisconsin, was founded in 1842 as a mission in the frontier and incorporated in 1847 as "a College of learning and piety." It is a seminary of the Episcopal Church in the Catholic Tradition.

[3] The School of Theology, University of the South, Sewanee, Tennessee, was established in 1878 and is situated atop the Cumberland Plateau on what some call "God's own Mountain."

visit at least two seminaries and one of them had to be Sewanee. I wrote
off to the eleven Episcopal seminaries for info and catalogues. My wife and
I were a bit stunned to find that almost all of them presented as graduate
theological schools, with little mention of Jesus Christ, worship, or piety.
There was one major exception: Nashotah House.

We loved everything about the Nashotah House catalogue and soon
found ourselves visiting there. From the first peals of the Angelus rung
from "Michael the Bell," I was captivated, hooked. As the saying goes, "All
this and heaven, too!" Amy loved it as well. In fact, just before our visit
ended I was asked by a senior seminarian if I'd made up my mind to come
there in the fall. I replied, "My wife has decided she wants to come here.
I'm still waiting for that 'still small voice.'" "That still small voice speaks
rather loudly through wives," he replied.

And so it was that we made our decision that Nashotah House was
where we had to be. The thing was, we still had to visit Sewanee. Even
though Nashotah was going to put us in the poor house, at least we'd made
our decision.

We visited Sewanee, and still preferred Nashotah. But thanks to
endowments, Sewanee was virtually free. No matter, we thought, we're
not going to let money make the decision for us. We went to all the inter-
views and services. Again, we preferred Nashotah House. By the time we'd
gotten half way home, money *had* changed our mind. We were going to
Sewanee.

Some time later I happened to pick up a book at the local mall: *Seven
Story Mountain*, by Thomas Merton. I'd never heard of him but the book
looked interesting. Therein I found Merton facing similar struggles with
his vocation. What did he do? He prayed, of course. But the peculiar thing
was that he offered some prayers to a saint, Thérèse of Lisieux.[4] He even
placed a rose at the base of her outdoor statue. What? This kind of spiri-

---

[4]Thérèse was born to a middle-class French family in 1873. Her father was a watch-
maker, her mother, who died of cancer when Thérèse was 4, was a lace maker. Thérèse was
cured from an illness at age eight when a statue of the Blessed Virgin Mary smiled at her.
She became a Carmelite nun at age 15 and defined her way to salvation and holiness as "The
Little Way." Her autobiography is entitled "Story of a Soul." She was declared a Doctor of the
Church in 1997 by Pope John Paul II.

tuality was totally foreign to me and I wanted to learn more. I was certain that I'd only be able to learn this type of piety at Nashotah House. Convincing my wife was a bit more difficult but, in the end, achievable.

Remember "Guru?" Well he'd long since moved away and converted to Orthodoxy. I had no idea what that was other than, apparently, a very exotic form of Christianity. I'd not seen him in years so, just before heading off to seminary in Wisconsin, my wife and I visited him in Florida. It was there that we attended our first Orthodox service, the Divine Liturgy, at a Greek Orthodox Church. It was, in a word: weird. People crossing themselves all the time; they had pews but rarely sat in them; I went to kneel—kneeling was forbidden I was told; everybody was kissing pictures. I thought my friend had lost his mind.

At the end of the service we went forward, like everyone else, to greet the priest. (It was actually to kiss the cross, but I didn't know that.) Upon meeting him, he gave me a piece of bread and my friend told me to kiss his hand. (This just kept getting stranger and stranger.) I did and began walking back up the aisle eating my little piece of bread when I noticed that several older Greek ladies were admonishing me about the crumbs—in Greek. Apparently, I was allowing them to fall on the floor. Gosh, get me out of here!

The following day Guru bought me *The Orthodox Church*, by Timothy Ware. I remember reading it on the beach thinking, "Yeah, right, beginning with the day of Pentecost an unbroken line of history!" It was a bit much. I consumed the book nonetheless. I also bought my first icon, "Not Made With Hands."[5]

Lo and behold, we ended up in Wisconsin at Nashotah House in the summer of 1989. Within fifteen minutes' drive from the seminary was a Carmelite monastery, Holy Hill. On our inaugural visit, I was bowled over. There stood a life-sized statue of St Thérèse; just like the one Thomas Merton prayed in front of in *Seven Storey Mountain*! The monastery even had a chapel dedicated to her. I was beginning, without cracking the first book, to learn about that piety.

---

[5]For more on the icon *Not Made With Hands*, see Appendix.

Our days at Nashotah House were both exhilarating and frustrating. I suppose all seminary experiences could be described in a like manner. The battle in those days, at that place, was over women's ordination. I was opposed to the idea upon entering the seminary. But then, due to friendships formed early, I warmed to the innovation by year's end.

The following summer I did my Clinical Pastoral Education (CPE)[6] work at the state mental hospital in Madison. Midsummer found me working on, among other things, honesty. By that I mean that I discovered that I was a "people pleaser" and afraid that in being truly honest I would alienate others. In this struggle, I came to realize that I was truly opposed to women's ordination, ordination of practicing homosexuals, and same-sex unions. I went to my CPE supervisor and told him of my self-discovery. What should I do? He suggested writing my bishop. "Always be honest with your bishop," he said. So I was.[7] I wrote my bishop stating:

> I am opposed to the ordination of women to the priesthood.[8] I am opposed to the ordination of an openly gay person [practicing homosexual]. Am I still welcome in the Diocese of Western North Carolina? Would you ordain someone with these convictions?

Later in the letter, I spoke of my struggle with these issues and the Episcopal Church's apparent acceptance of such:

> Do these issues arise out of the Holy Spirit's guidance? Or are they another attempt to make the Church more like the world? Society has remained the same—sinful. Yet, is it the mission of the Church to mirror society and affirm its nature? Is the Church supposed to keep a

---

[6]CPE: "Clinical Pastoral Education is interfaith professional education for ministry. It brings theological students and ministers of all faiths (pastors, priests, rabbis, imams and others) into supervised encounter with persons in crisis. Out of an intense involvement with persons in need, and the feedback from peers and teachers, students develop awareness of themselves as persons and of the needs of those to whom they minister. From theological reflection on specific human situations, they gain a new understanding of ministry. Within the interdisciplinary team process of helping persons, they develop skills in interpersonal and inter-professional relationships." *http://www.amerc.org/CPEclass.html* (accessed December 7, 2017)

[7]This was a different bishop than the one who sent me to seminary.

[8]For a note on the ordination of women, see Appendix.

close watch on science and society at all times to see what new finding or trend may end yesterday's sin?

Still wishing not to offend, I wrote "Confidential" on the outside of the envelope and asked that these positions be held in confidence between me and the bishop. His reply indicated his disappointment and invited further conversation upon my next visit home.

That Christmas break, the midpoint of my seminary experience, I received a phone call from a member of the Standing Committee, one of two advisory arms of the Diocese. Her recorded phone message gushed how she enjoyed my letter and agreed with my positions. Huh? Uh-oh! Obviously, the cat was out of the bag, just in time for the biannual meeting of the bishop, committees, and seminarians! To say that the road got a little rougher from that point on would be putting it mildly. I was still learning about that foreign form of piety.

In the summer of 1991 I attended the General Convention of the Episcopal Church in Phoenix, Arizona. I was sponsored by a traditionalist group, the Prayer Book Society,[9] and did communications work for them and the Episcopal Synod of America.[10] That Convention was a real eye opener for me. Never had I realized that so-called Catholics *voted* on their beliefs!

Bishop Frey of the Episcopal School for Ministry, Ambridge, Pennsylvania, was proposing an amendment stating that "sex outside of marriage is forbidden for priests and deacons." Both groups that I was working with supported the bishop's amendment. We published a daily newspaper of Convention events and opinions, as did the other side. When word got out that the homosexual lobby was going to support the Frey amendment, because they were then going to propose "gay marriage," the conservatives refashioned the wording of the amendment. It was changed to read, "Sex

[9]"The Prayer Book Society of the USA seeks to preserve for use and with understanding the classic and historic Prayer Book in its latest American edition of 1928. The Society is committed to the view that not only in its use of the traditional English language of prayer, but also in its forms of worship, prayer and doctrine it is one of the treasures of the Church of God in the West." *http://pbs1928.blogspot.com/2004/12/what-is-prayer-book-society-of-usa.htm* (accessed December 7, 2017)

[10]The *Episcopal Synod of America* (ESA) is a conservative organization of Anglicans which changed its name to *Forward in Faith—North America* in 1999.

outside of monogamous heterosexual marriage is forbidden for priest and deacon."

The day of the vote, the pro-homosexual lobby's publication stated there were some closeted homosexual bishops—one of whom was even HIV positive—and that if the Frey amendment passed, those bishops would be "outed." Unbelievably, the measure failed. I returned to seminary and told my wife that, with God's help, we would not die Episcopalian.

Early in my first year of seminary Guru sent me a prayer rope (*chotki*).[11] I remember receiving it at the little campus mail room and feeling a wonderfully bizarre feeling. Though new, the chotki seemed ancient. I learned the Jesus Prayer and would go to chapel 30 minutes before daily services to pray "The Prayer." I bought icons from the campus bookstore and placed them in my choir stall. I began to buy Orthodox books.

I also began to subscribe to Roman Catholic publications and purchase RC literature. I could not fathom actually becoming Orthodox, because I spoke only English. We'd visited the Greek Orthodox Church in Madison several times and the Serbian Orthodox Cathedral in Milwaukee. Both experiences were glorious, but foreign. Though my heart longed for Orthodoxy, my mind said that I might have to become a Roman Catholic in order to struggle toward salvation in my native, only, tongue. Survival within Anglicanism was becoming difficult, not to mention salvation.

There were rumblings on campus about a group of Evangelicals who had converted to Orthodoxy a few years earlier in 1987. There was also talk

[11]Many religious traditions make use of a set of beads or knots on a string as an aid to prayer. It is a way of connecting the activity of the mind and heart with the body. It can be used with any short prayer in a practice that can teach one to "abide in prayer", as the Apostle Paul taught. Over the course of centuries of ascetic Christian practice, the use of a simple phrase called the "Jesus Prayer" or "Prayer of the Heart" became identified with use of the Prayer Rope. This phrase is: "Lord Jesus Christ, Son of God, have mercy on me."

The prayer ropes are usually made of knotted wool yarn. The knot is a complicated one constructed of nine interlocking crosses. It was taught by an angel to a monk who was being troubled by the demons as he tried to complete his prayer rule. Orthodox prayer ropes usually have 33 knots, 50 knots, or 100 knots. Beads are often incorporated in the rope after every 10 or 25 knots. A cross and a tassel are usually attached to the rope. The knotting of prayer ropes is a common monastic activity, partly because Orthodox monastics make use of them as a primary "weapon" in the spiritual warfare. *http://www.shbyzantine.com/* (accessed December 7, 2017).

of a Western Rite[12] which was attracting like-minded Anglicans. Having never been of an "evangelical bent" and being captivated by the Byzantine rituals that I'd observed in my visits to Orthodox parishes, these discussions did not snag my attention. I did what many do: I collected Orthodox icons, books, prayers, and memories, all the while remaining within a Protestant communion.

After graduating from Nashotah House in the spring of 1992, I returned to my home diocese and was ordained deacon, and began serving my Curacy at an Anglo-Catholic parish in Asheville. I'd visited a couple times during my final year of seminary. The first time that I walked into the sacristy I was greeted by a four-foot statue of St Thérèse of Lisieux. That did it.

My relationship with the people in that parish was a blessing. They were a delightful and eclectic group of souls who relished Catholicism as understood by the West. They tolerated me filling my office walls with icons and my fascination with Orthodoxy. The Rector was a Francophile, and we were young and adventurous. So with his help we planned our first trip abroad, to France, for pilgrimage to Lisieux and other Catholic shrines.

Less than two weeks after the Church of England surprised the ecclesiastical world on November 11, 1992, and approved the ordination of women, my wife and I found ourselves on a plane headed for Paris. This was supposed to be a pleasure trip. But our adventure was pockmarked by my struggle with what to do next. My ordination to the priesthood was set for the feast of St John of the Cross, December 14, less than three weeks away. After the Phoenix convention, I'd said that we would not die Episcopalian. Suddenly death seemed nearer than ever.

We enjoyed our pilgrimage to France. My wife married a church nut. We visited: Chartes Cathedral, Sacre Couer, Notre Dame, Sainte Chappelle, Lisieux, and Lourdes. Our only Sunday found us worshiping in the Russian Orthodox Cathedral in Paris. About all I remember from that visit was that we showed up on time and were two of maybe five people in church. An hour and a half later, before service's end, we struggled to squeeze out the door, making our way through hundreds of people. Our

---

[12]For a note on the Western Rite, see Appendix.

French being limited, we thought maybe we'd misread the service times. Unbeknownst to us, we were being introduced to some of the struggles of "cradle Orthodoxy."

After about a year in the parish, it was time to make a decision. For personal reasons, the rector had been absent from the parish for several months. During his absence I had attended a conference for Episcopal clergy interested in Orthodoxy which was organized by some alumni of Nashotah House. In discussions with my wife, I had made the case that moving to another Episcopalian parish, given our beliefs and Anglicanism's direction, would seem hypocritical. Various events eventually brought things to a head and, in the end, I had Amy's total support to leave the Episcopal Church. She was, however, less than enthusiastic about Eastern Orthodoxy.[13]

Still not knowing how to properly go about things and very much desiring a change, I wrote a letter and mailed it to the Metropolitans of the Antiochian Archdiocese[14] and the Orthodox Church in America (OCA).[15] I'd heard that these two groups allowed for, and supported, the

[13]For my wife, Orthodox worship was beautiful but different, even bizarre compared to what she'd known. Yet when she saw "Orthodoxy in English" she was much more amenable and enthusiastic toward the faith.

[14] Antiochian Archdiocese: "A pioneer in the use of the English language in the Orthodox churches in the New World, the Antiochian Archdiocese has since 1917 kept in print and available Isabel Hapgood's pioneering English Service Book; it printed the first English music books for choirs in the 1920s; and its Father Seraphim Nassar produced in 1938 the first . . . comprehensive collection of texts needed for the chanting of complete services in English (The Book of Divine Prayers and Services). A full-fledged publishing department was established in 1940, and it has produced and distributed numerous titles in religious education, sacred music, and liturgical services." *http://antiochian.org/archdiocesehistory* (accessed August 11, 2017)

[15]OCA: "The Orthodox Church in America was originally founded as a mission and later became a diocese in the Orthodox Church of Russia, uniting in its fold Orthodox Christians of various national backgrounds and traditions. It subsequently developed into a self-governing Metropolitanate, the Russian Orthodox Greek Catholic Church of America. Confirmation as an Autocephalous Church was accomplished by the action of the Patriarch and Holy Synod of Russia on April 10, 1970. The Orthodox Church in America was proclaimed an Autocephalous Church on October 19, 1970, at the sessions of the All-American Council held at St Tikhon's Monastery in South Canaan, Pennsylvania." Preamble to the former Statute of the OCA, *https://oca.org/cdn/files/PDF/official/2011-statute-rev-final.pdf* (accessed December 7, 2017)

use of English in their services. The letter stated that I was about to burst, wanted to be Orthodox, and thought that an English speaking Orthodox mission might do well in our area. The Antiochians responded within four days. I made contact with Bishop Antoun and, at his suggestion, with Fathers Peter Gillquist and Gordon Walker. In reality, I had no idea what I was doing nor where it would lead.

In the Anglo-Catholic parish where I served, there was a shrine to the Blessed Virgin Mary. At the shrine, there was a bank of votive candles, a perpetual lamp hung from the ceiling, as well as a perpetual spotlight which illumined the statue of Our Lady. The Lady Shrine was usually adorned with flowers and sometimes her statue was even draped with various elaborate cloths. As an old Episcopal priest friend said, "If it's worth doing, it's worth overdoing." In the case of this shrine, well, you get the picture.

Directly across the nave from the shrine to Our Lady was a simple statue of St Joseph the Betrothed. One day, following my prayers at the Lady Shrine, I noticed the statue on my way into the sacristy. I looked at the three, only three, votive candles there. They were dusty, never used. On a whim, or so I thought, I decided to light a candle and say a prayer. Not knowing much about St Joseph, save the obvious, I ended up asking his aid in my struggle toward Orthodoxy. Looking back, I'm reminded of Thomas Merton and St Thérèse. Yet at the time, I was oblivious to all but the intensity of my struggle.

Through the daughter of a parishioner, an Orthodox convert, I learned that there was a Carpatho-Russian[16] Orthodox mission in the area. I rode out for a look-see only to discover the mission was dedicated to St Joseph. I was still oblivious. Within months of that simple prayer before St Joseph's unkempt shrine, so many things started happening, pushing me toward

---

[16]"The American Carpatho-Russian Orthodox Diocese was established in 1938 by His All-Holiness, the late Benjamin I, Ecumenical Patriarch of Constantinople, under the Patriarchal Seal in the official Patriarchal Document listed under Protocol No. 1379 and dated September 19, 1938, and was canonized in the name of the Holy Orthodox Church of Christ. The Diocese was incorporated in the Commonwealth of Pennsylvania in 1950." *http://www.acrod.org/diocese/about* (accessed December 7, 2017)

Orthodoxy that his heavenly intercessions could not be, in hindsight, denied. That insight was still some way off.

Upon the Rector's return, I asked for the weekend off. That Friday, with the allowance of the Carpatho-Russian priest, I spent 24 hours alone at St Joseph's Chapel: reading, praying, worrying. It "just so happened" that it was the Western feast day of St Joseph. My wife and I also went to the Greek Orthodox Church for Sunday's Liturgy. When the weekend was ended, I knew what I had to do.

In March of 1993, I visited the Greek Orthodox priest in Asheville and told him of my intentions to become Orthodox and start an English speaking Orthodox mission in Asheville. Though I was worried about his reaction, to my surprise he said, "Great! The more the merrier." He gave me a censer, censer stand, incense, charcoal, some books, and a list of non-Greek Orthodox folks that might be interested.

I renounced my Episcopalian Orders. Pascha, the following month, we were received into holy Orthodoxy by Fr Gordon Walker at St Ignatius of Antioch Orthodox Church, Franklin, Tennessee. On the night before our reception into the Church it dawned on me, dense that I am, that St Joseph had answered my prayer. I told Fr Gordon all my St Joseph connections and he said, "Then you should take the name Joseph." Amy Beth took Elizabeth, the mother of St John the Baptist, as her patron saint.[17]

Later, we began our first mission, the "Asheville Evangelical Orthodox Mission," in the South. The generic unorthodox sounding name was eventually changed, with the blessing of Metropolitan Philip, to St Nicholas Antiochian Orthodox Mission. We had reader's services, Typica,[18] in our den for 14 months. During that time, I completed the St Stephen's Course in Orthodox Theology. I was ordained deacon at the hands of Bishop Basil at St George Cathedral, Wichita, Kansas, and priest at the hands of Metropolitan Philip at the Parish Life Conference hosted by St George, Vicksburg, Mississippi—both in the spring of 1994.

---

[17]My given name is David; my wife took the saint's name "Elizabeth" (mother of St John the Forerunner) because, having been unsuccessful in conceiving after six years of marriage, she thought she might be barren.

[18]Typica: An Orthodox worship service for laymen without clergy.

My story is not much different from the host of other stories of Americans converting to Eastern Orthodox Christianity. Ever seeking the Truth, all the while loving and serving the God of my youth, I found the faith thanks to a series of struggles, "coincidences," and the prayers of someone about whom I still know little, St Joseph the Betrothed. I am also, after all these years, just learning to struggle. In the following chapters I will list some of my struggles, your struggles, our struggles—the American struggles of converts, reverts, and retreads—within our new home: The Orthodox Church.

Your Story

4

Who's Converting & Why

Charismatics

Those coming to Orthodoxy from a Charismatic background are many. They are attracted by authority and new experiences. Charismatics depend heavily on the *charisma* of the pastor.[1] If he exhibits "openness to the Spirit," and has a dynamic personality, all the better. The flavor of Charismatic groups grows bland without newer and better experiences. This often leads to a form of "Charismania" where church services resemble religious pep rallies; the better the rally, the better the church. That kind of excitement is hard to sustain. So, they search.

Such heightened searching can lead further to what one minister termed "Cruise-mania." That is, in search of the newer and better, Charismatics often *cruise* from parish to parish. Which brings to mind one of their weaknesses: They're used to switching.

Also, given the nature of charismatic experiences, Charismatic "baggage" may linger, much like an accent, long after the chrism has dried. While baggage from previous affiliations is prevalent for all converts, it can be acute and pernicious with former Charismatics. They were fashioned that way, or naturally drawn to such, and must struggle mightily—and be directed with patience and understanding—in their struggle

---

[1]This *charisma* is usually a personality trait—as in "he has a charismatic personality." It should not necessarily be confused with the *charismata*, or spiritual gifts, which are bestowed freely by God's grace.

within the true faith. However, unlike a majority of American converts, those coming from a Charismatic background have fewer problems with the convert's temptation toward Orthodox "head knowledge."

Christian Culture Burn-outs

I served in the mountains of North Carolina for more than thirteen years. Believe it or not, Asheville was a haven for "dirt eating, tree hugging, Druids" (i.e., the different). From "alternative lifestyles" to blatant unabashed witchcraft, Western North Carolina had become a tainted magnet. Coupled with the conservative views of the homegrown locals, this wove an interesting tapestry. Within this demographic may be found those who long for Christ without so-called "fundamentalism."

Once, in my "previous life," a friend and I entered a Satanic Bookstore in Los Angeles. Having been a Christian all my life, I was curious. What nonsense! Without Christ, at least according to this shop, there would be no Satan worship. Practically everything within the store was merely anti-Christian. In some respects, tainted by youthful rebellion, I was disappointed.

The same scenario often conflicts the contemporary hippie seeking Truth. All else eventually proves to be a sham, a shell, a shadow of the Truth. The stereotype of Bible-thumping goodie-goods has helped some to abandon the faith of their youth in search of the exotic. Yet, their conscience nags them, beckoning them Christward. Many find that Orthodoxy wonderfully fills that void.

Anglicans (Episcopalians)

I'll admit, I'm suspicious of Anglicans just now jumping ship. This is probably a great dose of pride on my part. But, the Episcopal Church has changed so much just since I left that if someone is just now waking up, well, they've been comatose. It brings to mind the old joke:

> The Anglican bishopess is led into the church by half-dressed liturgical dancers and altar girls. She bears statues of Buddha and various

Hindu deities. The congregation sings Hare Krishna songs. The bishopess places the statues on the altar and turns to the congregation and invokes the Mother Goddess. In the pews, one old guy turns to his pal and says, "Harry, I tell you, one more thing like this and I'm outta here!"

Even so, Anglicans still come to Orthodoxy. Honestly, depending on their local circumstance, their hesitancy might be justifiable—even at this late date of Anglicanism's decline. For instance, one's home parish may be a far cry from the nuttiness manifest in more urban or "enlightened" areas. It is possible, especially in a "sane parish," to ignore the greater communion's wholesale abandonment of Christianity.

Many Episcopalians are moored in their version of Tradition and, because they're not used to it, are slow to change. Yet they've been forced to suffer the changes of women priests and bishops, the homosexual agenda, and endless liturgical innovations. Some eventually decide to see Christ without change. Many feel that they are truly "Coming Home." More than one Episcopalian has said "I didn't leave the Episcopal Church, it left me." With such folks, when Orthodoxy sticks, it sticks.

Back in seminary, a friend of mine was ordained before graduation. He and I had often commiserated about the sorry direction and various ills afflicting the Anglican Communion. We went out to dinner shortly after his ordination. When discussion turned in that direction, he was surprisingly silent. When asked, he pointed to his collar and said: "This changes things; now, when people talk about the Church, they're talking about me. The Church has suffered many heresies through the ages, it'll weather this storm."

Several years had passed when I learned that he had converted to Orthodoxy. I called; we talked, and I reminded him of that earlier justification. He replied: "What constitutes proper health care changes entirely when the hospital is on fire." In a nutshell, this is the plight of right believing Episcopalians.

Baptists (Protestants)

The South has a predominance of Baptists who are, in many ways, the epitome of Protestantism. Most Protestants are good, godly, morally-upright folks. Yet they come to Orthodoxy seeking The Real Deal. I once heard a priest say that Baptists already have "the right Lord and the right Book, now they just need to get in the right Church." There's truth to the saying, but not entirely. Most of them have a misunderstanding of the Lord (e.g., Incarnation, Redemption, Salvation), and they have only a major portion of the Bible and not the whole Book. Many Protestants, particularly Baptists, seem to revere the Bible itself as the Incarnate Word of God.

They also suffer from "Romophobia." That is, they fear things resembling Roman Catholicism. Yet the greatest struggle for many Protestants is letting go of the erroneous belief in "once saved, always saved."[2] If they truly convert (that is, continually convert), they make excellent and pious Orthodox Christians.

Many Protestants also struggle with authority. Having lived under "No Creed but the Bible," they may come to a point where honest questions lead to greater doubt or confusion. *Sola Scriptura*—Latin for "Scripture Alone"—is fundamental to their Christian upbringing. They often find more joy than most when they finally come home to the Church that gave us the Bible.

Lest we get too puffed up, we Orthodox should be mindful of these words from Fr Alexander Elchaninov: "On Protestantism and Orthodoxy: in the little things they have, they have obtained very great results, and we, who have very great things, vegetate in mediocrity."[3]

Roman Catholics

Essentially, Catholicism without a pope is what they seek. This is not to say that they disbelieve in the integrity or sanctity of the man holding the office of the papacy. Rather, many Roman Catholics come to

---

[2]For more on *Once Saved, Always Saved*, see Appendix.
[3]Elchaninov, p. 121.

appreciate the historical collegiality of the episcopacy found within the true Church.[4]

It's odd to report that many who come to Orthodoxy from the Roman Catholic communion do so because of Orthodoxy's "leniency." For example, the Orthodox Church does allow divorce and remarriage under appropriate canonical circumstances. Thus, in reality, many Roman Catholics find the Church after having suffered a great fall.

The legalistic splitting of hairs that dominates the scientific formulas of Roman Catholic theology has left many falling toward grace. Fr Alexander Elchaninov says: "One of the features which distinguish our theology from that of the Catholics is it does not look at things legalistically, but in terms of God's grace."[5]

There's the oft heard grumbling about the liturgical reforms following Vatican II. Vatican II resulted in some of the worst changes in the history of the Roman Catholicism. As a result of it, Catholics were allowed to become Protestants. Priests were encouraged to say Mass with their backside toward God and to celebrate the Eucharist using substandard language.

The Nones or Unchurched

Although hard for those born between 1946 and 1964—Baby Boomers—to fathom, many among the younger generation, especially those born after 1980, have never been exposed to Christian church life at all. When able to shed their indoctrinated hedonism, these seekers are often best equipped to drink deeply from the well of the Orthodox Christian faith.

During my summers in college, I sold books for the Southwestern Book Company. Each year, when recruiting others to go door-to-door, the often heard excuse was, "I have no sales experience." Southwestern's response was, "Great, that's even better! No experience is better than *bad* experience." In other words, learning and training can be hindered by

---

[4]Granted, in this country, in our day and age, such collegiality looks non-existent at worst, and messy at best. But a cursory study of church history will prove that it is indeed the way of the one true Church.

[5]Elchaninov, p. 54.

time wasted on unlearning and un-training. Converts without the burden of "Christian baggage" may have fewer struggles with their new-found faith and are often more open to the fullness of Orthodoxy without pre-conceived resistance, heterodox notions, etc.

Plain Ol' Kooks

Honestly, this category probably represents a great many converts. Reading over my own journey to Orthodoxy, I realize I might resemble this label more than I'd like to admit. I can't really define this group. Like many things in life, when it comes to kooks, you know one when you see one.

A dear friend from a long line of Episcopalians once commented: "For years I'd wondered where all the colorful characters had gone. After becoming Orthodox, I found them." As one priest said, "Shine a light bright enough and even the bugs will come!" Indeed. The problem is, not all bugs are alike—which makes this category a very broad one. Those who know, know. There's nothing quite like a Church Nut to make life interesting. Thanks be to God, the Orthodox Church is open to all—Fools for Christ, and just plain fools.

These seven groups—Charismatics, Burnouts, Anglicans, Baptists (Protestants), Roman Catholics, Unchurched, and Kooks—make up, in my experience, the majority of American seekers.

Retreads

Back when I made my initial call to an Orthodox bishop, I had been an Episcopal priest for only four months. I was more than nine years away from finally paying off my seminary bill. I wanted to become Orthodox. I still felt called to the ordained ministry. I asked His Grace what I should do. He said, "Well you'll have to go off to seminary." What! (I wasn't yet versed in Orthodox polity.) It was a Monday afternoon; I was calling from Asheville. I was nervous and certainly didn't want to hear that I was headed back to a seminary. The bishop suggested I visit him in Englewood. I said, "Sure, Your Grace. When?" He said he was available tomorrow, as in the very next day. "Uh . . . no." "How 'bout Thursday?" he said. (This wasn't working out too well.) He ended up putting me in touch with some elder convert clergy and, eventually, I enrolled in the St Stephen's Course of Orthodox Study and later, the Doctor of Ministry program. So it is that every year finds a new crop of retreads at Antiochian village and other jurisdictional training centers—being *Orthodoxized*.[6]

Retreads have a more difficult journey than most converts. As Pastors they are greatly attached, in a God-pleasing way, to their non-Orthodox flocks. In a less lofty fashion they are often encumbered by important but worldly concerns: salaries, scholarships, and pension funds. A man with a family in a mainline church may be fully aware of the cancerous state of his denomination and still be stuck. It is, as many have recounted, the most difficult and heart-wrenching decision of their lives. The married pastor's vocation as husband, father, and provider wars against his spiritual needs and his, and his family's, salvation. While this is true of many converts, the struggle is greatly magnified for potential retreads.

Reverts

The label "reverts" was coined on an Internet discussion list and refers to those who have been "born anew" within the very same faith in which they were baptized as babies. Because of cultural issues, often involving the liturgical language used in the divine services, many cradles either marry outside the faith or experience non-Orthodox Christianity *in English* once they move away from home. Reverts are those who have found their way back.

Because of the various languages and cultures present in this country, coupled with acculturation and mixed marriages, reverts are growing in number. As we move toward a genuinely "American culture," this category will only grow. Some churches are reluctant to change from the language and customs of their founders. It takes time. Change is difficult. (And, for some, it isn't necessary or prudent.) In the meantime, a goodly num-

---

[6]It seems so simple, looking back. But for clergy interested in becoming Orthodox, it can often seem like "you can't get there from here." For me, "here" was the South. Believe me, it's a place where, outside of certain ethnic enclaves, Eastern Orthodox is about as foreign as you can get.

ber of cradles have come *back* home to assist their home communities in this endeavor. Or in many cases, they choose to find an Orthodox community that teaches and worships in the language that they—and their children—understand.

One thing is certain and bears repeating: *You cannot be Orthodox alone.* Those who try to be Orthodox alone are handicapped. We work out our salvation in community. That community, the one that God provides for us, is full of sinners and will never be perfect in and of its individual members. The Church is a spiritual hospital. Communion is the medicine of immortality. Love is paramount. Converts to American Orthodoxy—cradles, retreads and reverts—struggle toward salvation together, intentionally, in community.

5

American Hurdles

Individualism

Political commentators and ideologues often attribute this country's greatness to the American spirit of "rugged individualism." That may or may not be true about the American experiment. However, pure individualism of any sort is contrary to the very nature of the Church. Individualism, being so ingrained in our American personalities, is a high hurdle to clear. As the saying goes, "We are damned alone; we are saved in community." Individualism, though popular within much of Protestantism, is counterproductive to one's salvation in the Church.

Orthodoxy does not rob us of our personalities, unique qualities, charismas, or talents any more than marriage refashions us as automatons. All we are called to do is to be faithful. Fidelity changes people. But it robs us of nothing except chaff, and helps us to be fruitful in Christ.

Authority

Americans are not used to authority. The very event of our nation's founding seems to rebel against hierarchy and authority. Our movies, songs, TV programs—our very American nature—is saturated with questioning and challenging authority; it's an American thing. While the freedoms of this great land, thank God, may allow us to worship as we choose, the character instilled by such freedoms often find conflicts with authority. Though surmountable, it is a hurdle nonetheless.

Prior to converting to Orthodoxy, many converts' experience of clergy was akin to their perception of some funeral home directors—sappy, available, present, and accommodating. The preacher might deliver a stinging message from time to time, but his or her presence is rarely an "intrusion" in the life of those in the pews. Certainly, he wasn't involved in their diet or calendar. He wasn't present when they confessed their sins on their pillow. The preacher was there to deliver the message on Sundays. He presided over weddings, funerals and, if applicable, baptisms. The preacher's authority was the Bible. Thus, within the Protestant milieu, authority was relative. Everyone had a Bible, the paper pope—especially the preacher who just talked about it in front of more people.

Standing

Americans will stand for 1.5 hours for a ride at Disney World; one hour to buy Christmas bargains at Walmart; 40 minutes for a good hot-dog. But try convincing them that standing for a long church service is good for their soul! I've actually witnessed people sitting through a goodly portion of Liturgy only to later stand in the parking lot, in one spot, talking for hours. Americans have their priorities. Sitting in church is one of them; an American norm.

The first time I visited an Orthodox church, I was confused as to why, with perfectly good pews, people sat so infrequently. This is one of the most common observations of newcomers to the church. Why do you stand so much? Pastors should be sensitive to the past experience of seekers, converts, and those with special needs. Harvests worth gathering have taken time and care to grow. And though it may look identical, no produce is exactly alike.

It should also be mentioned that some converts become fanatical standers. While it is traditional for Orthodox Temples to be pew-less, we live in a country where the majority of churches have pews. For an individual to make an issue of this by, literally, standing out in a crowd, can become divisive and destructive. As with any battle, you must choose the hill you want to die on. Learning to worship God in community without being a stumbling block to self and others is a battle-worthy cause. If you can sit or stand without judging those doing otherwise, glory to God! It may prove best, even God-pleasing, to follow the advice of St Ambrose to the mother of Blessed Augustine, St Monica: "When in Rome, do as the Romans do."[1]

Intellectualism

Americans suffer from too much head and not enough heart. "Heart" is not to be confused with the contemporary hysteria over our emotions. Rather, having been indoctrinated with all manner of knowledge in the sciences, Americans long for things spiritual: using their brain as a homing device. This can be misleading.

There is no higher learning than can be found within the treasury of holy Orthodoxy. But—ask any sailor—treasure may provide a trap. It is tempting for the seeker, even the priest, to get caught up in the head knowledge of Orthodoxy. Yet without heart, without love, without participating in the simple truths of the Gospel, we are lost at sea.

Many American Christians are used to a system of clear-cut and well-defined dogmas within their faith. Are these available in Eastern Orthodoxy? Absolutely! But knowledge won't save you. And, thanks to the expanse of a 2,000-year history, innumerable saints, and writings galore, it would be nearly impossible to digest all of the "head knowledge" of Orthodox Christianity in several lifetimes. As one convert said, "Before becoming Orthodox, I'd read all the books and knew all the teachings of my denomination; this is not possible in Orthodoxy." Breaking the habit of the intellectual pursuit of salvation can be joyous, freeing—and frustrating!

---

[1] The story is told that when St Monica visited Rome she was surprised that they fasted on Saturday before the Sunday Eucharist. She asked her pastor, St Ambrose, about this. He famously replied not to be concerned about it, but "When in Rome, do as the Romans do."

The Struggle with Struggle

In spiritual warfare, what we sometimes fail to realize is that *struggle* is good. If we are struggling, guided by right intent and an enlightened conscience,[2] we must understand that the struggle is good. Yet the world teaches us that struggle is bad. In our relationships, when Americans have a struggle—without the benefit of Christ and His Church, a pure intent seeking after righteousness, and a godly conscience—we make wrong decisions. In time, we come to believe that the struggle is bad. Every time there is a struggle, Americans are tempted either (1) to *numb* the struggle (through alcohol, excessive sleeping, drugs, the internet, video games, daydreaming, movies, and other methods of escapism) instead of fighting the godly fight; or (2) to get rid of the relationship that has, in our minds, caused us the struggle (e.g., divorce, damaged parent-child relationships, and broken friendships).

Also, in such a mobile society as ours, we don't necessarily *have* to form close relationships with anyone. Thanks to the phone, television, and internet, we have multiplied and magnified our separation all the more. Were we to surround ourselves with those whom God has given us (family, friends, neighbors, etc.) we might find the nature of the struggle to be different. That is, we tend to see ourselves in a truer light by those with whom we are in a relationship of mutual Christian love. Essentially, we should struggle as a family not as individuals.

Returning to my point, the struggle is good. We must begin with that in mind. *The struggle is good.* If someone confesses, "I still struggle with

---

[2]There is a more definitive term used in Orthodoxy, *nous*, meaning: "The eye of the heart." The nous has a relationship with God, it receives the energies of God; God reveals himself to the nous, while intelligence, as an energy, is that which formulates and expresses the experiences of the nous. Taken from Orthodox Psychotherapy–The Science of the Fathers, Hierotheos S. Vlachos (Livadia, Greece: Birth of the Theotokos Monastery, 1994), p. 107.

The adjective is *noetic*: referring to man's intellect. Not to be confused with man's rational faculty, the intellect is the means by which man, in a direct manner, is able to perceive spiritual realities. Taken from *Precious Vessels of the Holy Spirit–The Lives and Counsels of Contemporary Elders of Greece*, H. Middleton (Thessalonica: Protecting Veil Press, 2003), p. 201.

'X,'" the first thing that I have to remind myself, as priest and confessor, and that which I have to counsel the penitent is: The struggle is good. It must also be remembered that the enemy is not very original. The devil uses only what works. If we've fallen before because of a particular passion, most likely we'll be greatly tempted in that area again. Warfare is waged. Yet, where there is *no* struggle the battle is already won. Who do you think wins when we let down our guard? God forbid that we allow the Enemy this victory! It's when we *don't* struggle that we become complacent. We become desperate. We become depressed. We become despondent. We lose hope. Given our comfortable American society, appreciating the truth that *the struggle is good* is indeed a difficult hurdle.

Suffering

By and large, post WWII Americans have known little or no suffering. Suffering is generally thought to be bad, to be avoided. I once had a man ask me if suffering was necessary once he converted to Orthodoxy. Mind you, this was a man who'd been twice divorced, lost a child, and whose life was in a general malaise. Still, he wanted to know if suffering would *come* with Orthodoxy! What he didn't, perhaps couldn't, realize was that he'd been suffering all along without the grace of God imparted within the Church.

In May 1993, I gave a talk to Episcopalian clergy interested in Orthodoxy from the perspective of a recent convert. The questions were flying. For want of words, I said, "Once you become Orthodox, you may not have all the answers, you just won't have the same questions." Concerning suffering and Orthodoxy, I believe this holds true.

As Fr Alexander Elchaninov writes, "We should not invent our own sufferings."[3] In other words, "Don't go seeking crosses; the Lord will provide." Sufficient for the day is the Lord's provisions, both the struggles and the grace to overcome them.

Bearing one's cross takes on a whole new meaning within Orthodoxy. As a former Charismatic once joked: "Before I was Orthodox I used to

[3]Elchaninov, pp. 94–95.

point to certain people and think, 'You're going to Hell.' I became Orthodox and it suddenly dawned on me, 'Uh-oh, I'm going to Hell!'"

Those who've converted to Orthodoxy know the scoop: We must
work out our own salvation. We must be gentle with others, severe with
ourselves. Salvation is a selfish pursuit, won within community, within
the Body of Christ, the Church. Within this context, suffering takes on a
whole new meaning. "Glory to God for all things!"

Saturdays

In American society Wednesday is "hump day;" Friday is "TGIF." Of
course, in Orthodoxy, Wednesday is a fast day in remembrance of the
betrayal of our Lord; Friday we fast in remembrance of the crucifixion.
Most converts get used to this worldly feast/Church fast reversal. Just don't
mess with an American's weekend! Yet, isn't the reason for the traditional
Monday through Friday work week setting aside time for the weekend's
worship? A priest once recounted to me how he'd said, from the Ambo, "If
you're not in church on Saturday night, I know what you're doing: you're
watching TV!" More than likely, in America this is true.

It is a testament to the Judeo-Christian principles that once permeated
this great land that those two days, Saturday and Sunday, are set aside
from the normal work week. Helping Orthodox Christians prepare for
Sunday's worship by getting them to church for Saturday evening's service
is a struggle for all pastors, whether the parishioners are cradle or convert.
This struggle against sloth has always been prevalent. It's just news to new-
bies (and even some cradles) that Saturday is a church day too.

Fasting

By abstaining from feasting—and feasting foods—on certain weekdays
and seasons, Orthodox fasting seems very peculiar to Americans. The
term "fasting" conjures up notions of not eating at all; which is, of course,
allowed as a pious practice! But, when Orthodox Christians use the term,
it usually refers to abstinence from feasting foods (e.g., meat, fish, dairy,
wine and oil).

Also, outsiders don't understand why, when fasting, Orthodox can eat shrimp, lobster, or crab, but not Spam. Why can you eat expensive meals but must shun an 89-cent hot dog? Trying to instruct an American that we fast from feasting foods (meat, dairy, wine, oil) is quite a chore given the fact that whizzing through McDonald's drive-thru is considered a "sub-meal" and not viewed as feasting at all![4]

A 90-year-old parishioner once told me that the word "diet" is a modern concept. Back when he was growing up they ate potatoes. His mom had a dozen diverse ways to prepare potatoes. But they were certain, most every night, that they would be having potatoes for dinner. And, it should be added, they were happy for it! America has come a long way since then.

Non-Orthodox

Most American converts find themselves in awkward situations with their non-Orthodox friends and extended family members. Wednesdays and Fridays may not be as difficult to negotiate as is the Peter-and-Paul Fast, Western Easter, and Christmas. I once baptized a man who for years had hosted the family pig-picking on July 4th. Of course, that's within the (Julian Calendar) Peter-and-Paul Fast. But that was his one big family obligation. It was family tradition.

There is a rule of thumb concerning fasting and non-Orthodox friends and family: "Eat what's served you." But this rule can become a temptation. One couple, recently chrismated, moved away. The next major fast to come along, I called to see how they were doing. They, in jest I suppose, replied "Oh, we're doing fine. We're just eating over at our [non-Orthodox] friends' each evening!"

It's not only the fasting that presents a hurdle for American converts and their non-Orthodox relations: preparation for communion, confession, not attending non-Orthodox services, and a whole host of other oddities (not to mention the Theotokos) help to strain relations. With maturity in the faith, many converts come to learn that love is most

---

[4]Actually, we shouldn't be spending large amounts of money on food when fasting. One of the fruits of fasting is giving alms (of money saved) to the poor.

important. Many of the challenges presented by our non-Orthodox relations can be overcome with love. The temptation, at least in the beginning, is to try to justify bad behavior by catechizing our mom, grandmother, best friends, spouse, or mother-in-law, in the rightness of our new-found faith and practice. Such behavior bears little, if any, good fruit.

Gratification

More and more, Americans are accustomed to instant everything! What with microwaves, cell phones, email, fast food, and online services: We're not used to waiting. We hate it. Patience may be a virtue, for *you*. But (collectively we say), for *me*, I want it right *now*!

The Church doesn't work that way. God doesn't work that way. As evidenced in the following chapters, almost all our struggles toward and within Orthodoxy are compounded by our lack of patience and our lust for instant gratification. This is true of the human condition in general; it is especially true of Americans.

6

Convert Baggage & Struggles

Validation

The chief need of converts, that which many are seeking, seems to be validation. In my experience, most converts have been on a search for God, community, the Truth, holiness, or some other common good deemed essential to their salvation. They come to Orthodoxy still searching. While they found their previous experience to be less than the fullness of the faith, nonetheless, they want to be validated in themselves. It is a great temptation: *I'm right. I've always been right. Now I've found the true Church to validate my rightness.*

This can often lead to a form of delusion, or *prelest*,[1] hindering the convert's path toward humility by the constant temptation of super-correctness. That's why we pastors and parishioners alike must help them appreciate their path toward the faith instead of utterly rejecting it and their family and friends. Those previous experiences have helped to shape them and make them who they are. Just because it was outside the Church doesn't necessarily mean it was demonic. After all, God uses what works. If you are an astrologer, he guides you by a star to the manger. Helping converts affirm their "past life" is a step toward assisting them in the struggle against super-correctness. A retread once joked: "I believe converts shouldn't be allowed to speak on anything regarding the faith for at least ten years after their conversion."

[1] *Prelest* or *planē* (Illusion): literally "wandering" or "going astray;" the corruption of human nature through the acceptance by man of mirages mistaken for truth; accepting a delusion as reality. Taken from *The Art of Prayer: An Orthodox Anthology*, Igumen Chariton of Valamo, compiler (London: Faber & Faber, 1997).

For many converts "super-correctness" is oftentimes not only a temptation, but a condition! There's a certain kind of madness that tempts and often consumes some converts. Many have experienced what Fr Seraphim Rose called "crazy convert" ("CC") disease. This often defines those who wish to *get* something out of Orthodoxy.

> [She] will very likely not even remain Orthodox. There's nothing in it but coldness, criticism, and self-justification. It is a spiritual poison for her to live alone. She may not fall into some spectacular delusion, but pride will develop in her to unmanageable proportions. We have had experience with this type of "CC," and there just is no treatment for it. She could only be cured by real obedience, which is precisely what she cannot give.[2]

> Pray for *R*. He writes that he is about to "give up" on Orthodoxy and is "weary" from not having found what he has been searching for sixteen years. Sadly, a typical convert story (one of the basic types): emptiness inside, and he wants to get something from Orthodoxy without working on himself, i.e., giving something to God.[3]

The affliction of super-correctness befalls many converts; for most, it's only for a season. For some, unfortunately, it becomes a chronic part of their Orthodox canon. Trying to "out orthodox the Orthodox" becomes an endless pursuit which bears little fruit, is not right, and misses perfection. Practice does *not* make perfect. Practicing error, regardless of the number of repetitions, only perfects error. We are perfected in love. "Above all hold unfailing your love for one another, since love covers a multitude of sins" (1 Pet 4.8). Converts should err on this side of correctness.

AAA: Anselm, Augustine & Aquinas

Within the predominant theology of America and the West, the finger prints of three men are evident: Anselm, Augustine, and Aquinas. One

---

[2] Alexey Young, ed., *Letters from Father Seraphim* (Richfield Springs, NY: Nikodemus Orthodox Publication Society), pp. 130–131.

[3] Young, p. 155.

could certainly make the case for Calvin, Luther, and others, but the theology of the Three A's is everywhere.

The Anselmian doctrine of the *Atonement* permeates the popular Christianity of America and the West.[4] Those reared with such an understanding see this in the Old Testament and the New Testament. They hear it preached, time and again, from the pulpit: "An Angry God was finally appeased when he killed his Son, who went to Heaven, now we're saved." This can prove to be a continuously underlying struggle for the neophyte. Now I realize there are those reading these words and thinking, "That's not it at all." But, like Anglicans who convert to Orthodoxy only to be joyously unburdened from having to continually defend the actions of Henry VIII, no longer struggling to understand salvation through the eyes of Anselm is a huge breath of fresh air.

For many American Christians, the movie "Star Wars," especially the first three releases, is pure theology. That is, the yin-yang interpretation of the battle between Light and Darkness is how they understand spiritual warfare. This is a form of an ancient falsehood (heresy) known as *Manichaeism*.[5] Blessed Augustine was a Manichaean for nine years, and although he is revered as a saint of the Church, some of his writings are tainted, or interpreted, with vestiges of this error. His teaching, particularly concerning original sin and original guilt, permeates Western Christianity.[6]

Thomas Aquinas, known as the father of Scholasticism,[7] is the author of the *Summa Theologica*. His influence on Western Christians is best summed up in the following quotes:

> It is a vast generalization, but it is, nonetheless, therefore generally true, that the western mind: energetic, exploratory, analytical, systematic, rational and empirical, has made a Christianity of its own. One

---

[4]For more on *Atonement*, see Appendix.

[5]For more on *Manichaeism*, see Appendix.

[6]For more on *Original Sin & Guilt*, see Appendix.

[7]For more on *Scholasticism*, see Appendix. Many Orthodox (e.g., Fr Seraphim Rose) view the fruits of Scholasticism as an elevation of reason above faith and tradition. See Fr Seraphim Rose, *Genesis, Creation and Early Man: The Orthodox Christian Vision* (Platina, CA: St Herman of Alaska Brotherhood, 2000), p. 315 ff.

can trace a clear historical line in western theology from St. Augustine, through the scholasticism of Thomas Aquinas, to the crisis of the Reformation and the fragmentation into either a monarchical concept of papacy on the one hand, [or] the idea of every man his own pope on the other. In other words: the disintegration and loss for most people of the mystical sense of the *ecclesia*, the body of Christ, in any real form save that of an institution. Starting with our old friend in western theology, Thomas Aquinas, the Scriptures begin to be seen as a form of revelation; that God reveals himself to the reader, in some form, through the book. This idea, of course, is readily taken up, following the development of printing and the greater availability of books, in the Protestant Reformation. *Sola Scriptura* becomes the cry; the Bible as the one source of theological authority in the Protestant scheme of things, once set loose from the papal Magisterium.[8]

Practicality

Orthodox Christianity is very practical. By that I mean within a proper catholic context, it makes perfect sense to the senses of the faithful. St Vincent of Lerins defined "catholic" in the fifth century as "that which has been believed everywhere, always and by all."[9] As with all things practical, the faith is strongly rooted in the experience of those who have gone before us.

We struggle toward salvation in humility and with sacrifice. This is new to American converts. Within much of American Protestantism, pride is almost deemed a virtue. Salvation becomes a badge of honor, a guarantee for those puffed up with "knowledge" that they are already "saved." Evangelism is left to the individual. This "evangelism" is basically pointing out the errors of those being evangelized and providing correction that is also available through the "evangelist." When these people come to Orthodoxy, they are relieved of the "individual evangelist" role. To many, this

---

[8]From the website of "The Antiochian Orthodox Church in the United Kingdom and Ireland," in an article entitled, "An Orthodox View of Church History," by Fr Chrysostom MacDonnell. *http://www.antiochian-orthodox.co.uk/* (accessed August 11, 2017)

[9]For more on the *Vincentian Canon*, see Appendix.

had proved to be a heavy burden over their years as a Christian. Yet the pendulum may swing the opposite way and the temptation is to become intoxicated with the "mystical" side of Orthodoxy while eschewing the practical.

Orthodoxy, in its practicality, is incarnational: "God became man that man might become God" (St Athanasius the Great). Incarnational Christianity—in truth, there is no other kind—is foreign to many converts. There is this struggle with the notion that it's only "what's inside that's important." This may be a continual temptation for the neophyte. Reverencing icons and relics, making deep bows and prostrations, standing for long services and processions, abstinence from food and drink—are all good for one's salvation. These bodily forms of Orthopraxis[10] and worship affect the soul more than an outsider could ever imagine.

Of even greater importance is the practice of love, humility, and forgiveness. Sure, this is preached in all Christian, even non-Christian, communities. But when one is held accountable to such God-pleasing ideals by one's confessor, priest, and bishop (not to mention fellow brothers and sisters in Christ), it makes for a new struggle wholly different from feelings and feel-good worship. Orthodoxy is very practical, very simple, and, because of our stubborn self-will, very hard.

Marital Problems

As other Christian groups do not have the same understanding of marriage, divorce, and remarriage, many American converts come to the church with marital baggage in hand or clearly under the surface. Rarely have I baptized/chrismated a husband, and later children, and not the

[10]*Praxis:* the doing (e.g., Orthopraxis: the doing of Orthodoxy). "Every one then who hears these words of mine and does them will be like a wise man who built his house upon the rock; and the rain fell, and the floods came, and the winds blew and beat upon that house, but it did not fall, because it had been founded on the rock. And every one who hears these words of mine and does not do them will be like a foolish man who built his house upon the sand; and the rain fell, and the floods came, and the winds blew and beat against that house, and it fell; and great was the fall of it." (Mt 7.24–27). See *Living the Faith—The Praxis of Eastern Orthodox Ethics* by Stanley Samuel Harakas (Minneapolis: Light and Life Publishing, 1992).

wife. This has proven to be a burden and struggle for all involved. I don't recommend it. That said, on many more occasions, I have received husband and wife together only to discover the depth of their marital depravity afterwards. The danger here is that the priest and/or confessor may be seen as a partisan confidant in confession or counseling. This may lead to increased problems between the husband and wife, because often they may not have a correct appreciation of the nature of the mystery of confession. Orthodox priests must make it clear, early and often, to married converts—*before* reception into the Church—that areas of marital difficulty must be dealt with mutually and that the sacrament of confession is not the place to "win friends and influence people."

Sexuality

A convert's understanding of the nature of marriage is often flawed by their previous experience, as is their understanding of sex in general. Perhaps, in these latter days, this is true for all mankind: cradle, convert, and non-Orthodox alike. One thing is certain: other Christian groups do not teach sexual morality the same way as the Orthodox. Consequently, habits are developed that are nearly impossible for the neophyte to break. Married couples show up having continually practiced birth control. Singles show up with no experience of continence.[11] Married couples show up with no experience of abstinence. This is a great struggle that will not go away overnight. Forbearance, encouragement, continued counsel, and patience are called for.

I once heard of a priest who delivered a talk on sex in his church. He began by asking, "How many of you are *not* married?" After a showing of hands, he asked, "How many of you *are* married?" He then pointed from the latter group to the former stating, "All right, you can. You can't." This is true. God-pleasing sexual relations are between a man and a woman within the sacrament of holy matrimony. Period. Everything else is merely a footnote to that axiom.

---

[11]Continence: refraining from sexual intercourse or discharge of bodily fluids and/or masturbation.

Various Gnostic heresies believe that the soul alone is pure and the body is evil.[12] We do not believe this. Sex is not a sin. Sexual desires and feelings are not, in and of themselves, sinful. Our bodies are not evil. Christ the Savior saves the whole of mankind, including the body. It is the misuse of sex, the abuse of our bodies that is sinful. Our bodies are not our own. Having been redeemed by Christ, our body is the temple of the Holy Spirit. That which defiles the body also damages the soul.

Americans have hastened happily down a perilously slippery slope over the past fifty years. The Kinsey Report of the 1950s, the introduction of the birth control pill in the 1960s, the sexual revolution, the drug/disco era of the 1970s, the spread of AIDS in the 1980s, the homosexual propaganda of the 1990s, and, in general, the wholesale discarding of self-control and moral standards over the past twenty years, has landed us within a cesspool of tangled bodies and confused minds. This perverse insanity has even infected many people claiming to be Christians.

A priest once told of a man who came to see him about becoming Orthodox. The priest said, "Okay, we'll need to discuss who Christ is, the Church, the sacraments. . . ." The man interrupted him saying, "I'm gay." The priest said, "Okay. But if you want to become Orthodox, we'll need to discuss who Christ is, the Church, the sacraments. . . ." "Damn it! Didn't you hear me? I said I'm gay!" "I heard you," said the priest, "but if you want to become Orthodox, we'll need to talk about who Christ is, the Church, the sacraments." Crying, the man told the priest that other pastors had either told him it didn't matter, or to get out! It took the man a couple years to become Orthodox, but another ten years to become celibate. He claims

---

[12]Gnosticism: the doctrine of salvation by knowledge. (This definition is based on the etymology of the word: *gnosis* "knowledge"; *gnostic* is the adjectival form of the word.)

"[Gnosticism is a] collective name for a large number of greatly-varying and pantheistic-idealistic sects, which flourished from some time before the Christian Era down to the fifth century, and which, while borrowing the phraseology and some of the tenets of the chief religions of the day, and especially Christianity, held matter to be a deterioration of spirit, and the whole universe a depravation of the Deity, and taught the ultimate end of all being to be the overcoming of the grossness of matter and the return to the Parent-Spirit, which return they held to be inaugurated and facilitated by the appearance of some God-sent Saviour." *http://www.newadvent.org/cathen/06592a.htm* (accessed August 11, 2017).

he could never have made it without the benefit of Christ, the Church, and the sacraments.

"Troglodox"—Orthodox Troglodytes

You've seen them. The man grows long hair and beard, forgets how to smile. The woman covers herself from head to toe. Her modesty smothers her dignity. They both stop bathing. There's no visible joy in their life. Their wrists are covered with wool knots. They eat only broccoli; tofu is reserved for feast days. They begin shopping for a home—preferably a tent or a lean-to—out in the woods, sans the burden of electricity.

These things may not be harmful in and of themselves. Yet oftentimes, when converts confuse such "asceticism" with Orthodoxy, it can have dire results. This "devolution" is often viewed as a sort of "monasticism." Though they may exhibit some of the same characteristics, monastics are usually working out their salvation in community and under obedience of a spiritual father.

"Troglodox" are often alone, a married couple, or paired with a few others of like mind. Unlike their monastic brothers and sisters, they are most often not following their ascetical path on the advice of their spiritual father and the tradition of the Church, but in spite of it.

Name That Convert, Calendar, or Quirk

It was Christmas, December 25, when Fr Tom's phone rang. Chad Whitley, formerly known as Rusty, had been gone from the parish for more than two years and, having read the Caller ID, Father was delighted to see his call. He greeted him: "Christ is Born!" Instead of the complimentary response, "Glorify him," his former parishioner said, "Not so fast, Father; not yet, he isn't." Father chuckled and said, "What are you talking about Chad? You haven't gone and joined the Old Calendarists have you?" "Actually, Father, I have. Oh, and I now go by Theoctistos," said Chad.

Though based on a true story, that example is a bit extreme. However, given the complicated recipe of Orthodox jurisdictional soup in America, stranger things have happened. Knowing what to call an Orthodox Christian, particularly a convert, can be difficult. It's often easier to negotiate cradle waters when it comes to names. For example, "Gus" often denotes a Greek man named Constantine. "Bill" is often used for an Arab man baptized as "Basil." Some Russians call "Vladimir" "Wally." Etc.

Yet converts go nuts over new names. It is customary in much of Orthodox culture to take a saint's name at one's baptism. This is done by the parents and godparents for babies, and by adult converts in conjunction with their priest. It is a wonderful custom, but it is not universal (e.g., Serbians generally have a patron saint for their family rather than a specific saint chosen for each individual). I've met many cradle Orthodox who have always received sacraments under their very American-sounding names. I've also encountered converts who won't speak to their non-Orthodox parents because they refuse to call them by their new name!

It is possible for converts to major in the minors on certain issues. It may not be the calendar or names. As always, the devil uses what works. If he can snare us into being intoxicated with portions of piety, that's all the better—for him. It might be head-coverings, beards, chotkis, prostrations (all worthy within the correct context) or a combination of exotic quirks that snags the convert toward madness.

How Do Orthodox Define "Weird"?

Fr Gregory lived next door to the church. He'd always believed that churches should be left open for prayer and, coming home with his family late one night, he noticed some candles burning next door. Before retiring, he went down to the church to make sure everything was okay. He was surprised to find the entire church filled with smoke and a man he'd never seen before sitting in the lotus position meditating. A parishioner, a recent convert, was over by one of the icons making furious prostrations, with a hand censer burning away on the floor by the icon stand. The convert was embarrassed at being discovered. And, when Father explained to him that normally people just come in and light a candle to say their prayers—and not burn unblessed incense in the church—the convert apologized and agreed to comply in the future. He also explained to the priest that though his friend (still in the lotus position and looking like he was in a trance) was not a Christian, he'd told him it was okay to come in here to pray.

Stories like these make cradles nuts. Perhaps it helps to explain why those who are raised in the faith are less prone to run after gurus, hippies, and kooks. Don't get me wrong. There are Bad Apple cradles, sometimes among the clergy, that cause great temptation for many a convert. But, for some reason, converts often find it hard to discern the line between pious and nutty.

I once went to a monastery to make my confession. My regular confessor was out of town and, having heard "rave reviews" about the clairvoyance of a new Russian monk there, I asked a blessing to go to "Fr X." During confession, after I'd mentioned a few sins, this "clairvoyant" began to chastise me for a particular habit that was not mine. He went on and on for about ten minutes before I interrupted him, "But, Father, I don't do that." He said, "Oh. Sorry. Okay, continue." I was less enthusiastic about his spiritual counsel from that moment on.

Some converts, unable to distinguish "Orthodox" from "weird," believe: the hairier the better, the dirtier the better, the smellier the better, the weirder the better. True, there are exceptions that prove the rule; but generally, it just isn't so. When we get away from the simple teachings of the Gospel of Christ and begin complicating matters with widgy-widgy and kookiness, we've begun eating a porridge that's less than salvific.

7

Other Temptations

Cradles

T hrough Catechism, reading of the Fathers, and other instruction, converts fashion an ideal Orthodoxy toward which to struggle. Then, they might get to know some of the "cradle Orthodox" only to be turned off. This can develop into a dichotomy leading to judgmentalism, pharisaism, and a sort of Convert-Superior-Orthodoxy which is far from the ideal!

We must all struggle toward salvation in humility. Thanks to the lackadaisical piety of some cradles, this can present a great challenge. To the eyes of the beginner, many cradles seem lax in piety, dress, service attendance, fasting, and Orthodox zeal versus ethnic identity. These can be a great temptation.

Fr Peter, a retread, and his wife once went to dinner with a Greek priest and his wife, both cradles. It was during the Great Fast of Lent. The converts ordered vegetarian pasta dishes, and the cradles both ordered steak. The priest's wife exclaimed: "Oh, I love converts! They fast!"

Different couple, different dinner: The priest's wife says, "I bet your people receive communion every week. Am I right?" "Well, yes, most of them do," said the retread, "but they're all very regular with services and confession." Unfazed she said, "I bet they eat meat on Saturday! You cannot receive communion unless you have fasted from meat for three or four days! Meat causes a fire in your belly." Not sure of what to say, the retread changed the subject.

Stories of converts being scandalized by the practices and perceived ignorance of cradles abound. But, brothers and sisters, really it works both ways. Perhaps a story will shed light on our communal plight:

In one parish, there was a disagreement about whether to do bows from the waist or full prostrations during the services of the Great Fast (Lent). Some said that during the holy season, at appointed times, all present must make a full prostration (kneeling, face to the ground). Others were just as adamant about bows from the waist being the traditional way. The situation intensified to the point that parishioners were not only yelling at each other, but almost coming to blows.

Finally, someone suggested that they go visit the hermit, Elder Zosimas, who lived in the forest. His age, experience, and wisdom would surely guide them to the ancient way of the Church. So, off they went to see the Elder.

When they found him, both sides related, with great emotion, their respective positions: some said bows, others said prostrations. Getting carried away in their zeal, and almost coming to blows in front of the Elder, they ceased fighting long enough to ask: "Holy Father, as you see, during this holy season of Lent, we have almost come to blows, our parish is being rent at the seams, we are at war with each other. Tell us, what is the ancient way of the Church?"

The Elder looked at them with tears streaming down his face, his heart aching, and said: "But, my dear children, this *is* the ancient way of the Church!"

Confession & Communion

A misunderstanding of confession—often fashioned by Roman Catholicism and/or the secular media—coupled with their previous experience of "communion," encourages converts to want communion whenever it is offered. Even if it is local parish or jurisdiction practice to require confession prior to each reception, converts may *still* be there every time. This can be a malfunction of piety and a misuse of the mysteries. As one priest related "In our parish we have 'partiers' who come to confession on Saturday and Communion on Sunday, only to start the party all over again on Sunday evening." Of course, this is abusive and counterproductive, possibly even damning. On the other hand, many cradles swing from the pendulum in the opposite direction.

> The ordinary year of a "normal" Orthodox: a "good" confession, a certain elation during half that day. The next day he slips already, but stops and recollects himself. An hour (or a day) later, he sins again. He recollects himself, but with less energy. And so one thing succeeds another, till he shrugs his shoulders and sinks into a hopeless callousness for the rest of the year, till Lent comes round again. Then he once more takes himself in hand, remembers the impending devotions, and so on. Thus, only six or seven days out of the whole year are given to God and to the spiritual life.[1]

Pastors must help each person toward a God-pleasing mean between these extremes. Not all potions cure all ills and some people are less well than others. Recognizing the need to visit a doctor and visiting a doctor are two separate things. Coming to confession, in and of itself, is a humbling act for most people. Everyone is different, all need salvation. At the risk of "shoulding" on you, let me recommend: Penitents should repent of all things that separate them from God (as needed). Confessors should aid them toward spiritual health and salvation by helping them to repent (as needed). This takes time, humility, compassion, a lot of patience, and a whole lot of love.

The Confession Fix

On their way toward baptism/chrismation, catechumens fret over their upcoming confession. One man even joked: "I wanted to go to a hermit priest in a distant land, make confession, and just after absolution—shoot him dead. Then come back to America and only have to confess to killing a priest." Our fears leading up that initial, lifelong, confession can be overwhelming.

---

[1]Elchaninov, p. 115.

Yet most come away from the experience relieved, overjoyed even, at their new-found buoyancy, only to despair when they later fall into the same temptations, passions, and struggles. Often, they lose heart because confession did not fix them. They misunderstand repentance. Some have the mistaken notion that telling their sins to God in the presence of a priest is the remedy for what ails them. Rather, just like a visit to the doctor, it is what happens *following* that appointment that is supremely important to the life and health of the patient. Confession is not the conclusion of repentance. Rather, it is often the beginning. St Theophan the Recluse writes:

> Finally, frequent falls and blunders that beginners always have due to inexperience, ignorance, ineptitude, and sometimes even weaknesses, weigh heavily on his conscience and can be more onerous than the great sins committed in his former carelessness. He is like a child that falls as he begins to walk. Falls require cleansing, consequently—contrition, repentance, and tears. Therefore, we are commanded to repent every day and even every minute. God be merciful to me a sinner! This should be the ascetic's ceaseless prayer.[2]

However, the glorious thing about this struggle is found in these words of St Macarius of Egypt:

> In accordance with divine providence, the devil was not sent at once to the Gehenna assigned to him, but his sentence was postponed in order to let him test and try man's free will. In this way, he unintentionally fosters greater maturity and righteousness in the saints by promoting their patient endurance, and so is the cause of their greater glory; and, at the same time, through his malevolence and his scheming against the saints he justifies more fully his own punishment.[3]

---

[2] St Theophan the Recluse, *The Path to Salvation: A Manual of Spiritual Transformation* (Platina, CA: St Herman of Alaska Brotherhood, 1998), p. 217.

[3] G. E. H. Palmer et al., trans., ed., *The Philokalia*, Volume Three (London: Faber & Faber, 1984), p. 299.

It is a struggle for the convert to grasp the enemy's machinations in this new-found (or newly defined) spiritual warfare. Yet the rewards, even this side of the grave, are grace, peace, and joy.

There is another form of confession abuse. Much like the self-confessed lyrics of a rock star, some are tempted to become an exhibitionist during confession. For instance, contrition and humility are lacking in their tales. Telling the priest all the gory and prurient details of one's private moments and fantasies can be sinful in and of itself—not to mention the temptations provided for the priest!

Jurisdictionalism

The smorgasbord of Orthodox jurisdictions makes absolutely no sense to most converts. I was once told by a monk "All monks are in communion with each other." Though said in jest, very much like a tightly knit ethnic community that fellowships within its own ethnic world, the same can be said of American converts.

I have come to believe that the American problem of multi-jurisdictionalism is a sin. If there is one single reason that Orthodoxy is often referred to as the "best kept secret in America" it's undoubtedly due to the plethora of jurisdictions in the United States. As a priest said, "The reason we do not have Orthodox Unity in America is because we don't want it. When we actually want it, we will do whatever it takes to achieve it."

Ordination Envy

Almost every adult male I have ever baptized/chrismated has been afflicted with the disease of Ordination envy. I asked an experienced Russian Protodeacon if he'd encountered the same and he replied, "Only every man's baptism over the past 30 years." (This is an exaggeration, but nearly true.) Since the Orthodox Church also has minor orders, readers and subdeacons, the temptation for many men is compounded. For most male converts, this struggle soon passes given the rigors of the faith and God-pleasing *directed* participation within the community.

Back when I was discerning a "call to ministry" as an Episcopalian, I visited with my priest and basically wanted to know "where do I sign?" and "what next?" I can still see him playing at the piano, smiling and shaking his head. "Not so fast," he said, "I want to revitalize the church school and youth group first." I then said something silly like, "Oh, I'm not interested in that, I want to be a priest." He smirked a little, played louder, and over the years, thanks be to God, those ministries were revitalized.

There's much to be done in American Orthodoxy. Though worthwhile and necessary, America may not be as hungry for more subdeacons and readers as it is for the preaching of the gospel, the ark of salvation, and the medicine of immortality. In the lives of the saints one reads of countless laymen who have spread the net of the Kingdom. Sometimes, ordination envy can be a hindrance not only to evangelism, but to salvation.

Internet

Though the world wide web is a two-edged sword, many converts are finding Orthodoxy on the internet. This creates great challenges for the Church, challenges that I'm not sure we have a handle on. It was a simpler time when the parish priest and the church kiosk were the seeker's venues for answers. Today, folks can surf the internet and read all manner of things that use the word "Orthodox" and be just as blind as when they started, if not more so. Clergy—bishops, priests, and deacons—can tell the flock one thing, only for them to be misled by contrary opinions within and without their own jurisdiction on the internet. For some, the internet has become the authority; which essentially means that we are dealing with Orthodox communicants who are really Protestants, trusting in their own authority to find Truth outside the walls of the Church.

Alas, most of the chatter on the internet is but idle talk and gossip. We live in uncertain times. We are often confronted with the sin of gossip within and without the local parish, particularly concerning "church politics." Following, believing, and spreading rumors and gossip is, as ever, a great temptation. Fr Seraphim's advice, over thirty years ago, is pertinent today:

A good part of what has caused your confusion is, to speak bluntly, gossip, rumor, tales. Shame on you! This is that very "grapevine" that has so disturbed you— but don't let yourself get mixed up in it. It's all smoke with little if any substance. We could tell you fantastic tales which were confided to us as virtual certainties. If you're going to be upset, let it be from something you hear first-hand, and which concerns you. Everything else discount at least ninety-nine percent or forget entirely, or you will never have peace of mind.[4]

We who wish to remain in the true tradition of Orthodoxy will have to be zealous and firm in our Orthodoxy without being fanatics, and without presuming to teach our bishops what they should do.[5]

Good heavens! What is happening to people? How easily one gets dragged off the path of serving God into all kinds of factions and jealousies and attempts at revenge.[6]

[4]Young, p. 117.
[5]Young, p. 168.
[6]Young, p. 205.

8

Extreme Troubles

Spiritual Abuse

Some converts come to the Church after having suffered pastoral abuse. They are relieved that the Orthodox priest, their new pastor, is not the abuser. But given fallen nature, it may only be only a matter of time before that label, pastoral abuse, is transferred to their priest. With all due respect, this may be done with some justification.

Within their former Christian denomination, the pastor, in the eyes of the Church, held no real authority, thus, he (or she) lorded it over the flock. On the other hand, the Orthodox priest may think nothing of the seemingly normal counsel or directives given to such a person. Sometimes pastoral counsel may be interpreted as divine law, unbreakable, where the priest is seen as an authoritative guru and the newbie his faithful unerring disciple. If this is the case, uh-oh! No matter what you might hear, this is not the Orthodox way. Perhaps such a scenario should be presented, early on, to those who may be susceptible to this temptation.

Another problem lies with the dilemma of multiple jurisdictions in America. This foists an unhealthy "competition" upon both clergy and laity. For instance, a man may go to his confessor and clear his conscience. At that time, or over time, his confessor may give him some "spiritual medicine" pertaining to his struggle. It may happen that the man may not like the prescribed medicine and follow his temptation to another confessor. The latter may or may not be privy to what all has gone before and may, in addition, be tempted by the ungodly competition for souls among

American Orthodox. This form of abuse burns everyone and weakens the witness of the Church in a thirsty land.

Counsel-worn

Thanks to saturation of the science of psychology within our culture, even within Christian groups, many come to the Church a bit "counsel-worn." They've accumulated all the pop-psychology terms for their various ills and are ready to study the same within an Orthodox environment. This can lead to a sort of reverse psychology. That is, the convert layman, seeing himself as knowledgeable and accomplished in the terms and mechanics of modern psychology and counseling, may set out to teach the priest a thing or two concerning his struggles, his nature, the dilemma. This is a temptation for the convert and a trap for the priest. All forms of this sort of "counseling" must be reexamined within the empirical knowledge of the Fathers of the Church for a God-pleasing re-evaluation.

One only has to read classics such as *Ladder of Divine Ascent* and *Unseen Warfare*—or the Psalms for that matter—to realize that mankind has not changed. No matter how much psychological knowledge you have, without Christ and the Church, you are lost. Don't misunderstand, it is possible to blend the two disciplines; it's possible, but not essential. It is not recommended for seekers, inquirers, recent converts, and/or most priests.

Reactionary

Some converts become so hooked on things being right or Russian or ancient—or "convert"—that they progress no further within their spiritual journey than developing into a reactionary. Such strugglers are quick to point out the errors of others while maintaining what they believe to be their own version of "pure Orthodoxy." Sometimes they confuse being right with being righteous.

It is possible to major on the minors; to become a *Rudder*-thumper, memorizing the canons but forgetting the Gospel. The canons, or rules, governing the Church (compiled in the *Rudder*) are not meant to be misused by the laity. They are, however, a God-pleasing way of Church gover-nance with the understanding that, unless otherwise indicated, each and every rule is for a particular place and time.

Yet one often meets a convert whose whole spiritual life seems to be governed by one or more of the canons. These may mix with fantasy to tempt the convert into believing that without his canon-quoting help, the Church may just fall apart.

Antagonistic

Particularly within American Protestantism, there exists a latent (but per-nicious) anti-clericalism. This may be a form of "Romophobia" or that spirit of rugged individualism. Yet it often happens that the same folks who have left other groups because of judgments against the pastor find momentary solace within the confines of the Church only to fall into the same temptations of judgment once the "honeymoon" is over. These folks can be quite antagonistic. Some may overcome this temptation; others may not. An experienced Greek priest once told me: "Once a priest hater, always a priest hater."

In his book *Clergy Killers*, G. Lloyd Rediger goes so far as to list the needs of a Clergy Survival Kit:

1. Mace, cattle prod, grenade

2. Night-vision binoculars

3. Karate handbook

4. Gifts for appeasement: a pound of your flesh; a pint of your blood; a resignation letter (in disappearing ink!)

5. High barnyard boots (it gets deep!)

6. Decoding ring (to see the truth!)

7. Mine detector

8. Ferocious Halloween mask

9. Beeper (for support group)

10. Prayer beads

Pastors most learn survival skills, for they may encounter clergy killers. And if they do, noble intentions, Christian love, and negotiation
will not save them. Even if pastors are willing to sacrifice themselves,
they share responsibility for defending congregations, because clergy
killers are perfectly willing to destroy congregations in their efforts to
destroy pastors.[1]

When it comes to an antagonist, one bad apple really *can* spoil the
whole bunch. Inevitably, antagonists tend to attract followers, often esca-
lating the situation from a ripple to a tsunami. From the book, *Antagonists
in the Church*,[2] here's a list of reasons why folks follow antagonists:

- People sometimes mistake antagonists for activists.

- The truth is often far less exciting than lies and half-truths.

- Bad news is more exciting than good news.

- Some people are gullible, and antagonists take advantage of that.

- Some people tend to follow orders without question.

- Some people are intimidated by antagonists.

- Many persons just don't want to rock the boat.

- People follow antagonists to be one of the crowd.

- Some join antagonists as a way to express their own feelings.

- Others follow antagonists because of misguided loyalties.

---

[1]G. Lloyd Rediger, *Clergy Killers: Guidance for Pastors and Congregations Under Attack*
(Grover Heights, MN: Logos Productions, Inc., 1997), pp. 132–133.
  [2]Kenneth C. Haugk, *Antagonists in the Church: How to Identify and Deal with Destructive Conflict* (Minneapolis, MN: Augsburg Publishing House, 1988), pp. 38–39.

- Some follow antagonists because antagonists frequently make their followers feel important.

The priest is often not recognized unless he is on the cross. And in some communities, there's always one—or a handful—that will try to make sure he stays there. Yet these folks need salvation too. Thus, pastors must also minister to the antagonists. Believe me, it's not easy. As one priest said:

> *There are people so needy*
> *Who have so many problems . . .*
> *They think only the priest can fix them.*
> *And when that priest doesn't have all the answers—*
> *God help that priest!*

9

Convert Strengths

Knowledge

Though converts often bring theological baggage from their previous denominations, they also bring much that needs to be affirmed. One impressive area is Bible knowledge. I've known converts who have virtually memorized the Bible. This is a great asset in catechism classes where they can be called upon to fill in the footnotes. Converts, through their studies of the Church, may also possess knowledge of what constitutes false teachings even more than most cradles. And, though it can eventually reveal a negative side-effect, through "reading their way into the faith," many converts are extremely well versed in church history, theology, and practice.

Knowledge gleaned from years of experience—human church experience—is also valuable. Although the None's clean slate may be a blessing, converts with years of experience in the human struggles of parish life can also be a great asset. Politics is part of the human condition, there's no escaping it. Honoring the church life experience of others, which was mutually beneficial and God-pleasing, can go a long way into tapping the talents of the newly converted.

Giving

Another area of convert strength is: Giving. Many American converts were taught that tithing is the God-pleasing way to give money to the Church. The truth is, if everyone in your parish tithed, you'd most likely not need head taxes, exhausting fund raisers, or worrying how the bills will be paid. Converts can provide an example for those without such a worthy practice.

You may run into cradles, clergy and laity alike, who frown upon tithing. This seems odd to a convert. Chances are these folks worship in an endowed or impoverished parish which is happy just the way it is. But, what could possibly be wrong with tithing?[1]

> Bring the full tithes into the storehouse, that there may be food in my house; and thereby put me to the test, says the Lord of hosts, if I will not open the windows of heaven for you and pour down for you an overflowing blessing (Mal 3.10).

It is not only financially that converts excel in giving, but in time and talent as well. This can pose a real struggle for pastors. Like all such manic endeavors, the labors may greatly outnumber the noticeable harvest. Guiding, consoling, and encouraging converts in their giving is one way for the pastor to work out his own salvation. There is so much work to be done in America. On the other hand, helping the newbie to guard his peace is also a paramount need.

Zeal

Converts tend to be evangelical—wanting to spread the faith by witnessing the Truth to others. While their methods of Christian evangelism may be foreign to the Orthodox ethos and may quickly fade, nonetheless, if given parish-helping tasks of spreading the word about church events and other worthy endeavors, converts can be a great asset. St Theophan the Recluse writes:

> What success can one expect when there is no enthusiastic zeal for a Christian pleasing of God? If there is something that involves no labor, one is ready to do it; but as soon as one is required to do a little extra

---

[1] At one time, some "old country" systems automatically took a percentage of a person's pay to support the church (e.g., Russia). The time when this was an acceptable excuse for an American's poor monetary giving to the church is, as they say, history.

labor, or some kind of self-sacrifice, immediately one refuses, because one is unable to accomplish it oneself. For then there will be nothing to rely on that can move one to good deeds: self-pity will undermine all the foundations. And if any other motive besides the one mentioned becomes involved, it will make the good deed into a bad deed.[2]

And so, it is clear that without zeal a Christian is a poor Christian.[3]

The zeal of the neophyte needs to be directed or, in my experience, it does not last. In the beginning, converts tend to be extremely loyal, even sycophants. Their new found knowledge of the faith leads them to more services, great support (almost adoration) of the clergy, intense inner scrutiny, and many God-pleasing manifestations. By and large, this changes. In fact, to paraphrase a famous Roman Catholic, Fulton Sheen, "Zeal is that which yells 'Hosanna' on the first day of the week, and 'Crucify him!' by week's end."[4]

---

[2]St Theophan, p. 30.
[3]St Theophan, p. 31.
[4]Taken from *Life of Christ*, Fulton J. Sheen (New York: McGraw-Hill, 1958).

10

Convert Burnout

Two-year Itch

It was at a clergy gathering that I first heard of the *Two Year Itch*, but it wasn't about the laity. Rather, a priest was speaking about himself. Heads started to nod. All the retreads were familiar with the same struggles, at around the same time, in our journey within Orthodoxy. The benefit for clergy is that, given the nature of the vocation, with few exceptions, we're in it for life. For laity, the devil may gladly provide other options.

Many converts seem to suffer "burnout" within a couple years of their reception into the Church. Over time, the attraction of candles, incense, icons, vestments, a capella singing, etc., seems less appealing. The convert is left dry and wanting. Yet this may be just where God wants him or her to be! If they can overcome this dry spell, they are often better grounded to weather the struggles and joys of the life of faith. Regrettably, some do not make it.

Many American converts find themselves in small convert missions. As with any fledgling community, labor is intensive and resources are minimal. This can mean lots of work for a new Orthodox. The initial zeal which is manifest during the catechumenate and early days may soon wane as the taxation of time, talent, and treasure takes its toll.

I must add, from a pastor's standpoint, that often this dry spell is "involuntarily" self-imposed. After the convert gets over the inaugural awe of the faith, and this may never happen for some, but does for many, he or she may get slack. *Reversion after Conversion* is typical. By that I mean, the Newbie stops saying Orthodox prayers, or following a prayer rule, and goes back to just talking to God about concerns, wants, and fears. Having grown accustomed to the lives and witness of the saints, the convert may despair, "I'll never make the grade." Having discovered the priest and/or bishop is no magic man and has clay feet, the convert may stop struggling to *be* Orthodox and wallow in just *being* Orthodox.

This pattern may be a lifelong struggle with Christianity itself. When it manifests itself within the true faith, the Pearl of Great Price, it can be spiritual poison. The practice of Orthodoxy can be hard, but it's *really* a difficult path for the convert who participates nominally. A cradle Orthodox Christian may be able to "justify" minimal participation in the life of the Church. After all, it's easier when it's something you just do, have done, and will continue doing because it's a cultural or family thing. But when you've struggled to become Orthodox—often alienating friends, family, and co-workers—the burden of nominal participation plays havoc with the conscience, piety, and soul of the American convert. Eventually the temptation may arise: Why bother?

Voyeuristic

I once joked with a parishioner, a convert seven years in the faith, that the convert motto is often "More books! More books!" He added, "Less reading! Less reading!" This is true, as is: "More icons! More icons!"—"Less praying! Less praying!"

Upon finding this wonderful new wealth of spiritual information, a convert can become a connoisseur of Orthodox writings and iconography. Without proper guidance, he may become voyeuristic in his faith, observing the life of the Church from the outside through books, books, and more books, icons, etc. For some, particularly if they came from a Bible-memorization background, they may learn to proof-text the Fathers of the Church the same way they once did the Scriptures. This form of head-knowledge Orthodoxy may stifle empirical growth in the faith.

Another form of Orthodox voyeurism is represented by the internet, where one can spend many hours digesting every Orthodox opinion imaginable. Most of this has little or no bearing on the person's actual living the faith. I remember one of my seminary professors saying, "Don't think you're going to make seminarians out of your parishioners." Thanks in part to the internet, many converts are now becoming armchair priests and bishops. Lacking face-to-face questioning, conversation, and struggle, the convert becomes isolated from the very community that God has provided for his or her salvation.

Progress-less

After about a year or two, one often hears a convert say, "I'm not making any progress." The overwhelming flood of knowledge, emotions, and zeal has dwindled down to the day-to-day struggle toward salvation. This is of course where the convert needs to be, but it can be a real downer. After a while Orthodoxy seems hard. Or as one man told me: "It finally dawned on me that this *is* hard!"

Then again "no progress" is a perfectly fine position to be in. Much of Orthopraxis is inner work. We're not called to become smarter about our faith. We are called to repent. This inner work may feel like we're moving backwards at times. I remember lamenting to my confessor, also a retread, how I felt the weight of my sins, and realized more sins, more than ever. He asked if this weight had increased, year after year, since my conversion to Orthodoxy. When I said "Yes," he said that this was common with converts. "The more we grow in the faith, the more we see our own sinfulness." This is progress—just not the kind many converts are used to.

Consider an attic. If you go into an attic, intent on straightening and cleaning, a candle will help you to see the clutter. A flashlight will work even better. However, once you've gotten the attic all tidied up with your small wattage light, you might feel confident enough to throw open the curtains. Caution! When you do, and the sunlight pours in, you may see every little speck of dust floating before your eyes. God, in his mercy, allows us only a candle or flashlight upon our soul when we are in the process of conversion. Once we begin to work diligently on our salvation, he allows us more insight. Though frightening, this is a step in the right direction.

Following a clergy meeting where the bishop had insisted that the gathered retreads follow certain established and traditional practices of the Church, a friend said to me, "I don't think the bishop realizes that these men would storm Hell with a water pistol for him." In hindsight, I believe the bishop was aware of this. Nonetheless, out of his love for his clergy, for Christ, and for his bride, the Church, he encouraged those priests to be faithful—*to the Church*. This is the progress, the faith of the Church, against which the gates of Hell shall not prevail. If we remain faithful, we are making progress.

No Satisfaction

Famous last words of many converts: "I'm not getting anything out of all this!" Many who come to Orthodoxy are used to a form of worship where one attends church on Sunday in order get charged up—spiritually, intellectually, emotionally—for the week ahead. The church's worship fills a need in the individual. He or she attends church to "get something." Orthodoxy, in its form of worship and piety, requires sacrifice and humility. It is a different type of worship, a different struggle. This can become frustrating for those who are used to being on the receiving end of a spiritual high.

When folks outside of Orthodoxy think of the phrase, "Priesthood of all believers," usually they imagine an equality of mission in the spread of the Gospel and the moral life. Yet "priesthood" refers to one who sacrifices. Sacrifice is at the heart of Orthodox worship. A man on his way to Orthodoxy, a potential retread, once told me that when he became Orthodox he might not seek ordination because it didn't feel necessary. All his life, growing up Roman Catholic and Episcopalian, he felt he needed to be the one up front leading the service in order to fulfill his ministry. Yet when he worshiped within an Orthodox setting, he felt every bit a part of the "experience" as the one up front, the priest, leading the service.

This is the reason we all face the same way, East, during our prayers in church. We are the people of God, the priesthood of all believers, offering our sacrifice of praise and worship to the Great High Priest, Christ the Lord. Ultimately, it is in this sacrifice that we find satisfaction.

Vulnerability

Learning to love is hard. Learning to love following a broken heart or abuse is harder still. In their quest for the Truth, some converts become dispirited. Nursing wounds, egos, and confusing emotions, many make up their minds to never wind up in such a state again. Yet look at the Man on the cross. It is impossible to love without being vulnerable. With or without Orthodoxy, this is a great struggle. It is impossible to be Orthodox without love. Given the struggle to love and, for many, a series of broken relationships with others—pastors, parishes, and denominations—converts may be more guarded than necessary. This may take time. Only fools rush in, even to the true faith.

To protect themselves from further harm, some wrap themselves in Canons and "Church Law" as a substitution for love. This is a sure sign of spiritual insecurity which, given its nature, may only be realized through maturity and personal experience. Sometimes this growth only happens after humiliation. As one priest related, "Struggle toward humility or suffer humiliation. The former is a whole lot better than the latter!" Either way, love of God and neighbor is paramount if we are to make it to the Kingdom. No amount of law, save the law of love, will save us.

While it is not my intent in this little book to offer remedies for every convert malady, it is true that without love we are lost. I believe I stand on God-pleasing ground in saying: "Love is the most important thing." When we forget this, when we lose sight of what we are about, we lose hope. Believe it: without love we'll never get to Heaven. It requires us to be vulnerable. Yes, we'll get our heart broken; it's a struggle. It is the most important struggle. Be faithful!

I'd Rather Switch

Why are some converts so easily tempted to run from one church to another? The answer may be as simple as: *They're used to switching.*

Believe it or not, some newcomers eventually view the Pearl of Great Price, the Church, in the same light as their previous affiliations. They discover their new parish is made of the same old sinners as their former.

Their priest or bishop, they soon find, is human and prone to error. They discover that *they* are the same old sinners. After a while, usually following some struggle, they conceive that the "statute of limitations" has run out and it is time to move on. Christian term limits. Some come to the deluded conclusion "Father's not a Starets.[1] Bishop's not a Starets. I'm the only Starets!" And they go their way, still searching. Paraphrasing a saying about lawyers, it is also true of Orthodox: "He who has himself as a spiritual father has a fool for a spiritual father."

Given the plethora of Orthodox jurisdictions in America, it's easy for converts to move to another Orthodox community. Sometimes this may be best for all involved; but when clergy do it, it's a whole different story. In most cases, this is done through canonical norms. Yet some retreads, viewing themselves as St Mark of Ephesus,[2] leave their bishop for perceived greener pastures. Upon leaving their rightful bishop for another, "more correct" one, these retreads (especially if they bring a group in with them) are often hailed by their new jurisdiction as heroes of the faith. "Ah! Look at the great sacrifice they have made!" But remember, obedience is better than sacrifice.[3] The God-pleasing reasons for clergy to abandon their bishop are few, grave, and rare.[4]

---

[1]Starets (sometimes spelled *staretz*): a holy person, often a monk or hermit (not necessarily a priest), gifted with the charism of spiritual direction in the Church.

[2]Our father among the saints Mark of Ephesus (Evgenikos), Pillar of Orthodoxy, was famous for his courageous defense of Orthodoxy at the *Council of Florence* (1439 A.D.) in spite of the emperor and the pope of Rome. He held Rome to be in schism and heresy for its acceptance of the *Filioque* clause added to the *Nicene-Constantinopolitan Creed* and for the claims of the papacy to universal jurisdiction over the Church, and was thus the only Eastern bishop to refuse to sign the decrees of the council. He died peacefully in the year 1452 A.D. On his death bed, Mark implored Gregory, his disciple, and later Patriarch Gennadius, to be careful of the snares of the West and to defend Orthodoxy. See *Address of St Mark of Ephesus on the Day of his Death,* quoted at *http://www.stjohnthebaptist.org.au/en/articles/mark.html* (accessed September 2017). For the *Council of Florence*, *Filioque,* and *Nicene-Constantinopolitan Creed*, see Appendix.

[3]"And Samuel said, 'Has the LORD as great delight in burnt offerings and sacrifices, as in obeying the voice of the LORD? Behold, to obey is better than sacrifice, and to hearken than the fat of rams.'" (1 Sam 15.22).

[4]For more on *Apostolic Canon XXXI*, see Appendix.

Godparents

One of the greatest struggles for a priest, especially in a convert mission, is assigning pious sponsors for those entering the Church. It's sad but true; many Orthodox converts eventually fall away from the Church. A goodly number of converts, especially in convert missions, have sponsors who have become "nominal" or even fallen away. Oftentimes it is better to assign a godparent outside the parish, someone who has proven to be stable and faithful. This abrogates the traditional understanding of the relationship yet, God willing, bears more fruit. (Perhaps, as the mission grows, more suitable sponsors will be available.) Do not make "buddies" godparents! Just as best friends often make terrible roommates, it is often the same with spiritual affinity.

I'd Rather Fight Than Switch

Let's be real, sometimes it's best if some people *do* leave the parish. This is especially true in the case of antagonists in fledgling convert missions. With parishes founded upon a single cradle Orthodox culture, a firm "family foundation" already exists wherein there are folks intent on weathering any and all storms together. However, communities with a convert base are often less solidly united. They are often glued together by doctrine versus blood and may suffer human politics within the Church badly.

Here are some words of wisdom from a *Manual for Missions:*[5]

> Beginning a mission is fraught with many, many difficulties and uncertain and unpredictable circumstances. Any potential priest should be a man who is not easily discouraged. He should be strong in faith and should have a positive outlook about the future. Further he must be one who is not easily threatened or intimidated and one who believes that God has led him to do the work he is doing.

---

[5]"Bringing America to Orthodoxy—A Manual," published by the Department of Missions and Evangelism, Antiochian Archdiocese of North America, Very Reverend Peter Gillquist, ed. (1997).

In my experience, whether a man is used to discouragement or not, he's bound for a good measure of it. Being a missionary in one's native land is heartbreaking. Staying positive is paramount. The evangelization of America is a worthy and, no doubt, God-pleasing pursuit for those who have found the Pearl of Great Price (often at great price). Weather the storm! The Lord provides. He provides both the storm, and the calming of the same.[6] Be vigilant. The simple fact that someone converts to Orthodoxy does not mean that they will not eventually turn and try to destroy the priest and parish that once welcomed them home. This is the nature of the struggle within these shores, outside paradise. Persevere!

Nominal Christians are welcome at the mission, but should not be given any major leadership role in the planning of the new mission.

How hard this is! One of the struggles for the retread mission priest is discerning leadership in the fledgling community. It's often easier to make a "silk purse out of a sow's ear" than to distinguish between a nominal Christian on fire for Orthodox evangelism and a has-been in search of a new playing field. Why? Because missions are so desperate for growth that a warm body is often viewed as covering a multitude of sins.

A mission sometimes attracts the disgruntled ex-members of other churches. Some may move quickly to the fore and act with authority. Kindly listen, but do not allow them to control the situation.

Here, in my experience—both personal and with other mission priests—is the essence of the retread's cross. As mentioned earlier, many men are laboring in fields where other Orthodox feared to tread, till, plant, and water. Yet when a cradle Orthodox comes along, one with lifelong experience and "success" in the Church, the temptation for a retread can be more than ample. There's only one Savior. Again, there are plenty of folks more than willing to see the priest nailed to the cross; but, he (you) is not the Savior. For mission priests wha are retreads, it helps to remember that the new cradle arrival in the parish is not the Savior either. In the most God-pleasing situations, the revert and the cradle can be honest and

---

[6]See, for example, the Book of Job.

up-front about this struggle from the beginning and till, plant, and water together. To avoid disaster, there is no other way.

All forms of nominalism must be discouraged from spreading to any new converts or new members.

Honestly, this can be difficult with missions that begin with a sporadic dose of cradles. First off, in remote areas, the cradles may not have practiced the Orthodox faith in a long time. In such cases, they too must be viewed as converts. One course of action is: *Education. Education. Education.* No, it won't save you. But it sure helps to buttress the evangelistic efforts of the fledgling community. The priest must be an educated man. By that I certainly don't mean a scholar, nor necessarily an alumnus of a seminary. He must strive to know God. He must know the faith. He must be able to transmit his knowledge of Christ, the Church, the faith—to the faithful. He must struggle toward God-pleasing wisdom and discernment.

Once at a gathering of Protestant clergy interested in Orthodoxy, the question was asked: "Why is it that some of the Orthodox clergy have no formal theological education?" The bishop answered, "I'd much rather have a priest who prays than one who reads." The sentiment here was not disparaging education. Rather, the knowledge of the priest must be founded and fed by his participation in prayer.

Here are a few more words of encouragement for missions:

Teach and preach to the faithful, but always with an open door to new commitments from those not living a spiritual life.

Work with those who seem to have a heart for God and are nominal out of ignorance.

And these, from Fr Seraphim Rose:

Pray for us. The mission fields are still open, and we should labor while there is still time.[7]

Continue in your God-given path, and sow the seeds of Orthodoxy wherever you can.[8]

[7] Young, p. 200.
[8] Young, p. 112.

While God tolerates our existence, let us try to be fruitful![9]

The Twice Converted

This category refers to those who have come to believe that their particular priest, bishop, or parish is just not kosher enough. Their solution is to jump ship—usually to a smaller boat. In the smaller boat, which the twice converted believe to be purer, there exists a great attraction: Correctness. Often this correctness is only a mask for design flaws. But for those seeking salvation by super-correctness, this seems to be a most fit vessel no matter the size or pedigree.

The twice converted may go so far as to seek reentry by way of baptism—whether or not they received Orthodox baptism at their reception into the Church. They may, yet again, change their patron saint (i.e., their name). Or, given their newfound zeal they may finally get "Barsanuphius" or some such placed on their Driver's License and other official documents.

The twice converted may look on the rest of the Orthodox as the great unwashed. Those who have only known the Julian Calendar (Russians, Serbians, etc.) are never quite as zealous about it as the twice converted. In fact, zeal is at the very heart of this group. They are "evangelists" seeking to convert all and sundry to the glories of rigidity. In and of itself, this will not save you.

Such groups tend to be overly obsessed with the Apocalypse, Chiliasm,[10] ecumenism, etc. So much so that, it seems, *virtue* is all but forgotten. The only virtue present seems to be one of separation. Most communicants within twice converted settings are retreads from another, or more than one, jurisdiction of Orthodoxy. It's like the old joke: A priest happens upon a deserted island only to find one man and two churches. Upon inquiry, the islander says: "Oh, yes. That's my church—and that one over there is the church I used to attend."

[9]Young, p. 133.
[10]*Chiliasm* comes from the Greek χιλιάς *khilias*, 'thousand,' and is defined by the *Oxford English Dictionary* as "the doctrine of the millenium; the opinion that Christ will reign in bodily presence on earth for a thousand years."

Our Story

11

Our Mission

One thing we must not forget: Orthodoxy *is* Christianity. It is tempting for us, even pastors, to fall into the trap of believing that Orthodoxy is an "add on" to whatever other form of Christianity was previously practiced. This is false. I used to view all the followers of Christ outside of the Church as, in a sense, catechumens; no longer. More fruit is borne when instruction and catechism start from scratch, teaching Orthodoxy. You cannot add Orthodoxy to Christianity. Rather, it *is* Christianity. We shouldn't beat others over the head with this fact, but we should never shy away from it.

Pastors should also beware of lame answers to good questions. The chief good question is: "How does Orthodoxy differ from, say, the Baptists?" The tempting lame answer is: "Oh, to a Protestant outsider it would probably look Roman Catholic." Wrong, unless you're in a Byzantine Rite Roman Catholic parish, Orthodox worship looks like no other. True, in its Western Rite expression, it shows similarities with Roman Catholic and Anglican worship. But, hopefully, when the seeker asks the question we're not going to confuse them with discussing different rites, etc.

Orthodox Christianity is the Church

All other manifestations of "church" have subtracted from the Church. Given my background in the Baptist tradition, I heard the Epistles anew, seemingly for the first time, when I became Orthodox. St Paul was writing to the Church. And here I was, now a member of that same body, the Church, hearing his writings in a whole new light. No longer did I have to struggle to hear the writings of St Paul speaking to me personally. From time to time that may be the case, yet the Epistles were and are to the Church. It is a "we" thing that we take personally; it's hard to explain to an outsider. But like all families, clarity comes within the confines of family membership. There's no other way to experience marriage and family than participating in it.

Not utilizing the whole of the canon of catechism and the Scriptures in teaching seekers about the faith is a mistake. It is incorrect to view all outsiders as catechumens. Converts need to reexamine, on their own terms, previously held beliefs and assumptions about Christ, the Church, and salvation. For the Orthodox to assume that those coming to her from other Christian backgrounds need merely to add icons, incense, and liturgical worship is an erroneous assumption. It is best to just start from scratch. "Scratch," in this case, is that faith which has been *preserved* and handed down from generation to generation in the Church.

12

Land of the Salt-Free God

With fads, eating trends, and all manner of diets, we Americans have proven that, for physical benefit, we can have discipline when it comes to our menus. But unfortunately, we've created a sort of "Health Cult" that the Church Fathers would find contrary to the faith. It has even affected our understanding of Scripture.

You are the salt of the earth (Mt 5.13a).

Salt is receiving a bad name these days. In our attempt to live longer and longer, clinging to this earth as if it were our final destination, we have thrown the salt out with the well water. Given this modern day, existentialist view of salt—how are we to understand the words of our Lord concerning this common seasoning? Maybe he should have said, "You are the beta carotene of the world?" Or, "You are the ThighMasters™ of the universe?" Or, "You are the whole bran, gluten-free substance of some-such?" Instead, God said "You are salt." Thus, salt can't be all bad. What's good about it?

Important since prehistoric times as a seasoning agent, salt preserves food and was commonly used in the religious rites of the Greeks, Romans, Hebrews, and Christians. It was an important medium of exchange in commerce across the Mediterranean, Aegean, and Adriatic seas. Salt cakes served as money in ancient Ethiopia and Tibet. The English word "salary" was derived from *salarium*, the Latin term referring to the salt allotment issued to soldiers serving in the Roman army. The most familiar use of salt is as a seasoning. Salt is an essential constituent in the diet of humans and other warm-blooded animals. Salt is widely used as a preservative for meats.

Salt both preserves and gives season to food. What does it mean to be "the salt of the earth?" It means *preservation.* Priests of Christ's holy Church are to preserve themselves and the flock from decay. Like cured ham or the salt that preserves our vegetables and other foods, pastors must preserve the flock by word and deed. Heresies, like germs, dissolve beneath the saltiness of the preservation of faith. Preserving the faithful means keeping in what's good—and keeping out what's bad (e.g., forgiveness is good; gossip is bad). It sounds simple, but you know it isn't. Our Lord's commission comes with a warning:

> If salt has lost its taste, how shall its saltiness be restored? It is no longer good for anything except to be thrown out and trodden under foot by men (Mt 5.13).

As far as preserving the faith is concerned, bishops, priests, and teachers of the faith are to teach only that which the Church teaches. When we stray from the Tradition of the Church toward either our own opinion or the liberal tendencies of the Protestant sects, our *salt* has lost its taste. Our holy faith becomes bankrupt by our loss of savor. The gates of Hell shall not prevail against Christ's holy Church, yet how many have lost faith due to the blandness of their lukewarm faith, religion, pastor, or church?

Furthermore, we are *all* called to season the world by our word and our example—our *godly* word and example. What a shame if our salt is too spicy! What a pity if our witness is too bland! We must keep our eyes on the prize, all the while living a life that is pleasing—not to men, but to God. The Apostle Paul encourages us, saying:

> Conduct yourselves wisely toward outsiders, making the most of the time. Let your speech always be gracious, seasoned with salt, that you may know how you ought to answer every one (Col 4.5–6).

Salt is necessary for us to speak with the grace of Christ—preserving that which is good and true, keeping out that which is unholy. This is not the god that our secular, sin-saturated world seeks.

The media is constantly bombarding us with a *low salt version* of God. This god requires nothing of followers and is not offended by any lack of morality. This god preserves nothing—not the faith, nor the faithful. This god is not the God of revelation. Rather, this salt-free god, is the god of human secularism. There is no Hell; Heaven is for everyone. All you must do to be glorified by the salt-free god is live and die. This is the god that the culture of death serves.

The salt-free god, who stands for nothing holy and heavenly, encourages you to live life as if there were no tomorrow. When, however, tomorrow arrives and you are in pain, this god will painlessly help you end it all. Thus, having served this god fully all your days, spending your time in a stupor full of all the comforts of modern life, you pass quietly into the salt-free heaven (which is nonjudgmental) full of even more joys than you saturated yourself with while on earth. All of this is painless, sacrifice-less, and salt-free. (It can even be seen in some churches where *the culture*—Greek, Russian, Arab, etc.—*is preserved* while the Orthodox faith is sacrificed.)

The seduction of the false god is everywhere, as it has been since the Fall of Adam and Eve. Yet, this is not the God whom we serve. Rather, at the end of Vespers and Matins services, Orthodox Christians sing:

> *Preserve, O God, the holy Orthodox faith, and all Orthodox Christians, unto ages of ages!*

We are singing about *salt*. We are singing to the Almighty God and King who gives salt and light and all good things to preserve the hearts and minds of His most precious creation: you, me, all mankind. Preserve, preserve, preserve! God how we need *salt* in America! Though it stings our wounds, it heals our infirmities. Though it restricts our hedonism, it preserves our godliness. It sweetens our speech and limits our gossip. It gladdens the hearts of man and is pleasing to God. Without it we become lifeless, faithless—godless.

Americans are so concerned about physical diets. What about spiritual nutrients?

> And do not fear those who kill the body but cannot kill the soul; rather fear him who can destroy both soul and body in hell (Mt 10.28).

No, it is not the salt-free god that we should fear. Rather, with fear of God and faith and love let us draw near to the God of *salt*. Let us cling to him who preserves us as his own. Let us live our lives as the *salt of the earth*—to the Glory of God—for our salvation and the sake of all mankind.

13

Culture Wars

T he popular 2002 movie *My Big Fat Greek Wedding* is the story of a Greek woman who falls in love and comes to terms with her own heritage and identity on her way to the altar. Through humor and exaggeration, many Americans were introduced to cultural differences that many Greek Americans, laughing out loud, were all too familiar with. As one convert, who is happily married to a Greek woman, related: "I live that story . . . every day."

Culture is like opinions; everybody's got one. It is inescapable, natural, a given. While it's tempting for converts to fall into the habit of judging the cultures of those whose church they've joined, it's nowhere near God-pleasing. *All* cultures help to shape and define each person's reality. And, honestly, lacking a uniform American culture, converts tend to form their own convert culture within Orthodoxy.

A retread who had spent a lifetime with converts before being assigned to an "ethnic parish" said: "Converts want Bible study, catechism, and continual teaching on Orthodoxy. Cradles, on the other hand, want you to visit their dinner table, bless their homes, know their family, and be present for family milestones." He ended by saying, "It's all good."

We converts often act badly within our new family. Much of what has been said concerning the struggle with our intellect can lead us to be very judgmental of our new-found brothers and sisters in Christ. Can you imagine marrying into a family and feeling extremely blessed to do so, only to criticize and judge the family members harshly soon after the honeymoon has ended? It happens. It happens too often in Orthodoxy.

What many fail to understand is: Converts tend to form their own exclusive culture. This group is filled with just as many "cultural" do's, don'ts, and customs that few cradles—other than reverts—are allowed in. Remember the cradle's house with no icons? Friends, at one time the Huneycutt icon corner consisted of 38 individual icons. Add to this 2–3 icons in every room, pardon the pun, but you get the picture.

Convert culture is maximalistic when it comes to Orthodox customs. For instance, the priest's greeting or "secret handshake": Converts love that. Prostrations, cassocks, head coverings, hair—you name it! Some converts make a religion out of otherwise God-pleasing piety. Someone outside of this clique, such as most cradles, might feel unwelcome to join in. Or, worse yet, the cradles judge the converts just as harshly.

That said, there is a bit of convert frustration about culture which needs a hearing. We all should talk to each other, work together, listen. Otherwise, the cultural clashes may often be an obstacle to salvation within some communities.

14

Orthodoxy in Dixie

O ver the years I've learned a lot about the cultural differences that create at least one of the chasms that make the journey to Orthodoxy difficult for many Americans. Almost all converts have their own stories of cultural wars within and without their new-found faith. Here follow a few reflections from a Southerner.

I was reared in a small town near Charlotte, North Carolina. Growing up, I never met a Jew, much less a Muslim. Lutherans were rare enough in my hometown, much less Roman Catholics. Basically, we were Baptists and Methodists, blacks and whites. I'd never even heard of Orthodox Christianity until I was on my way to the Episcopal seminary in the 1980's. Come to think of it, I'll bet most folks in my hometown *still* have never heard of Orthodoxy.

No Orthodox jurisdiction ever sent missionaries to the South. Most converts have stumbled upon the faith only after many years of searching. If this were different, perhaps more progress would be apparent in bridging the gap between East and South. Like St Innocent who helped convert the natives of Alaska by "incarnating" their native faith thereby bringing them to Christ, would that someone had intentionally helped the South to grow out of its native Protestantism into the fullness of the Christian faith. Instead, many of the "ethnic churches" resemble Protestant churches with icons and the assimilation, in liturgics and piety, has moved away from traditional Orthodox practice toward Protestant norms. Such a vacuum allows converts to flounder toward the Kingdom while accumulating various practices from the smorgasbord of Orthodoxy in America. It also lends itself to parish and/or jurisdiction hopping in hopes of finding the fittest vessel, the most correct iconography, the willing guru, etc.

I have heard that the seminaries in Russia are bursting with future priests. We have a priest shortage in America; they may soon have a glut in Russia. It wouldn't surprise me if they sent some of those men to this country to evangelize. That would certainly wake us from our jurisdictional squabbling and anti-Christian stupor! Maybe our constant judging and nitpicking would be tempered by some honest to goodness evangelism?

We Southerners have many weaknesses. Paramount is our ingratiating spirit. We deliberately set out to gain others' favor by winsome actions. Hopelessly people-pleasing we are! Being "cut from this cloth," we also have a weakness for taking a man at his word. If you tell us that you're going to do something, we expect you'll do it. If you don't, there's a good chance that you'll lose our trust, permanently. This behavior will differ between Southerners and Southerners, and between Southerners and Outsiders. Like any ethnic group, we trust our own a while longer. Yet, to a Southerner, duplicity appears rampant in American Orthodoxy. Arabs, Russians, and other cultures are accustomed to hubris and other blustering within daily discourse. In the South, we expect it of politicians. We discourage it in decent folks. In the South, integrity is expected of church leaders. Having found the true faith we're confused by contradictory words and actions that often emanate from the various jurisdictional hierarchs.

When I first became Orthodox in the Antiochian jurisdiction, someone suggested that I read a book entitled *The Arab Mind* to get a sense of my newly adopted church culture. The book claimed that, in Arabic, the root word for eloquence and exaggeration is the same. An Arab may exaggerate to show machismo. For instance, a man may shout across a street corner to another "I hate you." The other man replies, "I not only hate you, I'm going to kill you!" The man retorts, "I'm going to kill you *and* your family!" And so on. These same men may later be found sharing a friendly meal together. Words fail me in describing how this same dialogue might have ended in the South.

Contrary to outsiders' perceptions, Southerners do not put on airs. We may be hospitable, friendly, and civil, but what you see is what you get. If we share openly with you, it means we trust you. Once you break that trust, it may be irreparable. All are welcomed here. Yet, we are easily offended. If offended, the offending party will be cut off till reparation. Our people-pleasing nature lends itself to over sensitivity. It just comes with the territory. In the South, admiration comes easy, respect is earned over time.

Like all those outside paradise, Southerners gossip. In a region where being idle is considered a virtue, idle talk ain't far behind! I don't mean the kind of vindictive gossip popularized by soap operas and other media, though we have that too. Rather, Southerners carry on conversations in a way that others might view as gossiping. And, God help us, at times it is. Yet, often this is a manner of couching subjects within an engaging tale. It's the way we talk around here.

Southerners are self-effacing. We can take criticism if it's properly couched in civility or humor. If direct confrontation is necessary, things have already gone too far! Sometimes our neighbors to the North skip all the niceties and cut right to the chase. And, since all the Orthodox jurisdictions hail from a different culture with the "home offices" up north, this element of cultural war persists within church dynamics. Brutal honesty is not only unwelcome but most often rejected in the South.

Before attending my first gathering of clergy and church wardens in the Russian Church, I was asked about the nature and agenda of the meeting. I said, "Well, they'll probably argue and yell at each other for a few hours and then we'll have lunch. After lunch, they'll argue and yell some more then we'll kiss each other goodbye and go home." I'm no prophet, but boy was I ever on the mark with that prediction. In such a setting, you can recognize the Southerner: he's the one with his mouth shut. If asked, if honest, he'd say "I think you all are crazy." But, "don't ask, don't tell" has always been policy where I'm from. Being slightly dishonest in the name of civility is considered a virtue.

You yell at a Southerner and it may have eternal consequences. When we speak, all that's required of you is to listen politely until it's your turn.

We don't take kindly: yelling, interruption, jeering, or public ridicule. We may not break bread with you until there's resolution. You don't have to agree, mind you, but you must behave in such a way that assures civil discussion and debate. It may be that we take things personally. But, we operate on the assumption that *you do too*. Therefore, quite selfishly, the Golden Rule applies no matter your rank or station.

Northerners are most often defined by their family's nation of origin. This type of identification is foreign to the South where folks are generally identified by their family name and/or their religious affiliation. I've often heard Northerners speak of someone as Italian, Ukrainian, German, etc. Along with this description is the implied religion of those being described (Roman Catholic, Orthodox, Lutheran, etc.). This is not the case in the South. In the South, folks are defined by their religion: Baptist, Episcopalian, Methodist, Charismatic. So it is that Northern Orthodox are often amazed that Christians would intentionally convert to Eastern Orthodoxy. What an idea! Can you convert from Italian to German?

Folks in the rural South usually attend the church nearest their home. In the country, you will find mostly Baptists, Methodists, and Pentecostals. Towns will have Presbyterian and Episcopalian churches. Here and there, you will find Lutheran pockets and an occasional Roman Catholic Church. Latins and Lutherans may have a bit of a drive or live within a "family burb." Presbyterian and especially Episcopalian churches are populated with many who have "worked their way up" to that denomination. Your brand of Christianity may be a status symbol in the South. Unfortunately, viewed from such binoculars, Orthodoxy can seem a step down. Forgive me, but to a proper Episcopalian, Orthodoxy can seem downright barbaric.

When expected, don't be surprised if a Southerner shows up early and leaves late. We don't understand "Orthodox Time." If you tell a Southerner that something starts at 6:00 p.m., he'll most likely arrive at 5:45. We don't want to miss a thing. We're not only unaccustomed to the Orthodox habit of being late; we find it rude and uncivilized. Also, Southerners usually don't leave without saying goodbye, many times. This process of departing may take thirty minutes or more.

Southern culture is, at least, as relevant as other forms of ethnicity—whether "Orthodox" or not. We converts appreciate the foods and festivities of our adopted culture. But must we discard our norms and ways and replace them with those of traditionally Orthodox lands? Fundraising is fine, but what about tithing? Lamb's good, but so is pork barbecue. Pascha and kulich[1] is festive, but that first bite of pecan pie is just as heavenly. Can such revered Southern gatherings as Mother's Day, Thanksgiving, family reunions, BBQs, and oyster roasts be "baptized" into Orthodoxy? It's too early to tell. Orthodoxy is new to the South. It's yet to be seen whether the two—Dixie and Orthodoxy—can melt into one God-pleasing flavor.

So, what's a Southern Orthodox convert to do? Assimilation with the Protestant milieu is not an option. Been there, was that. Christianity *plus* icons and Typicon is not the answer. Why bother? Becoming a dirt-eating-tree-hugging druid is not the way. I mean, really! Then again, these options are all alive and "well" within the Church. And that may be okay, as far as God's concerned, but it comes close to grits without salt for a Southerner.

Thanks to the War Between the States and Reconstruction, Southerners have a strong distrust of outside authority. As the saying goes, "Fool me once, shame on you; fool me twice, shame on me." There's an underdog thread that binds us together. Yet when asked to perform a task by those in authority, one can bet it will be done. We are teachable. However, all things must be in accord with proper respect. Our experience teaches that there's virtue in losing when done graciously. Nevertheless, we have strong suspicions regarding authority. Those in positions of Orthodox leadership would do well to familiarize themselves with the norms of Southern behavior and expectations. After all, if you are serious about evangelizing another land, which the South definitely is, you would do no less!

This is not to say that the South should secede from the ethnic Orthodoxy of the North or of the Old Country. Rather, Southern Orthodoxy

---

[1]Pascha (often called "cheese pascha") and Kulich (accent on the last syllable): the terms refer to two Easter foods from the Russian tradition; Pascha is made from rich dairy products and eggs, and kulich is a type of egg-bread; recipes for both can be found on line. The pascha is usually spread on the kulich.

should be allowed to flourish with its own personality and character with proper hierarchical oversight. Any community that can appreciate this and encourage Southerners toward the Kingdom within their own *Southern* culture will do well in making solid converts to the faith in Dixie.

I say these things about my own native culture in light of the paradigms[2] provided by the Protestant theologian Neibuhr outlined below.

---

[2]*Paradigm*: a set of common beliefs and agreements . . . about how problems should be understood and addressed [Kuhn, 1962]. *See: https://plato.stanford.edu/entries/thomaskuhn/* (accessed August 11, 2017)

15

Culture & Theosis

A close relative to the Scandal of Jurisdictions is what might be termed, "paradigm pressure." If we imagine one's jurisdiction as railroad tracks, with the rails serving as paradigm walls, it is between these rails where the convert practices his or her faith.

For cradles, the rails are the rails and switching tracks is out of the question. Yet most converts have made a gut-wrenching decision to be on those particular rails, often losing jobs and friends in the process. When those rails seem to be heading in the wrong direction, the convert wonders if this was all a mistake. For some, the struggle is not necessarily against an ethnic Orthodox culture, but with Western culture itself.

H. Richard Niebuhr's classic paradigms of the interaction of Christ and culture may prove beneficial in the American struggle toward Orthodoxy. In his Christian classic, Niebuhr outlined five categories, or paradigms, of Christ and culture:

1) Christ against culture

2) Christ of culture

3) Christ above culture

4) Christ and culture in Paradox

5) Christ the Transformer of culture

Though written within a non-Orthodox setting, Niebuhr's paradigms can help us to understand our human struggle within the Church and the part which culture plays. Converting to Orthodoxy is hard enough.

Oftentimes the community in which converts worship is immersed in a culture foreign to their own. The following examples are not intended to cover the various ethnic cultures found within Orthodoxy. Rather, in general, they offer a lens for American converts, in whatever culture they find themselves, to view their own struggle toward salvation and the heavenly culture, the Kingdom of God.

Christ Against Culture

> Whatever may be the customs of the society in which the Christian lives, and whatever the human achievements it conserves, Christ is seen as opposed to them, so that He confronts men with the challenge of an "either-or" decision.[1]

From a broad perspective, we see this paradigm operating with certain fundamentalist groups. However, the convert may be especially tempted by this model—eschewing family gatherings, secular celebrations, and all manner of things in deference to his newfound faith. The choice for the convert is either the Church or the world. The world is viewed as the Great Satan and the Church, ever dwindling in size of the saved, is forever opposed to the ways and customs of the world. The convert may lump all other Christians, even Orthodox Christians within other jurisdictions, in this same "world" category. This is all done in the name of correctness. The Church (even in her human expression) is viewed as being perfect and pure, and it is the job of each individual convert to bear the mantle of protector and save the Church from the ways of the world and wayward Christians. A heretic is spotted under every bush, especially if he wears a miter. The Church survived for 2,000 years without that convert—but what of it?

[1]H. Richard Niebuhr, *Christ and Culture* (New York: Harper & Row, 1951), p. 40.

The Christ of Culture

In this group, Christ appears as a great hero of human culture history; His life and teachings are regarded as the greatest human achievement; in Him, it is believed, the aspirations of men toward their values are brought to a point of culmination; He confirms what is best in the past, and guides the process of civilization to its proper goal. Moreover, He is part of culture in the sense that He Himself is part of the social heritage that must be transmitted and conserved. In our time answers of this kind are given by Christians who note the close relation between Christianity and Western civilization, between Jesus' teachings or the teachings about him and democratic institutions.[2]

In an American context, lacking an Orthodox foundation, this category resembles something less than fullness and joy. It defines what we'll call "Secular Christianity." In this form, Christ is a good and moral teacher but not the Way, the Truth, and the Life.[3] He is all love and acceptance, sans judgment and accountability. He is not seen as God in the Flesh.

Given the historically monarchical nature of Orthodoxy, it's not as easy to wrap the Church in the Flag as some Protestant denominations are apt to do. In our day, this paradigm may be more tempting for cradles (e.g., Greeks, Arabs, Russians) than to converts. Yet in this case, they may mix culture with Church to the point where the lines are blurred. For example, everything must be Russian or it's not Orthodox. Greek civilization may be inseparable from understanding of the faith, etc.

Many converts are tempted by this cradle appreciation of "foreign" culture and may become *more* Russian than the Russians, *more* Greek than the Greeks, *more* Arab than the Arabs, *more* monastic than the monks, etc. I have even heard converts who begin speaking with a foreign accent as if that makes them sound more Orthodox! By the way, what is the Orthodox accent?

---

[2]Niebuhr, p. 41.

[3]Jesus said to him, "I am the way, and the truth, and the life; no one comes to the Father, but by me" (Jn 14.6).

Christ Above Culture

> This group views Christ as the fulfillment of cultural aspirations and the restorer of the institutions of true society. Yet there is in Him something that neither arises out of culture nor contributes directly to it. He is discontinuous as well as continuous with social life and its culture. The latter, indeed, leads men to Christ, yet only in so preliminary a fashion that a great leap is necessary if men are to reach Him or, better, true culture is not possible unless beyond all human achievement, all human search for values, all human society. Christ enters into life from above with gifts which human aspiration has not envisioned and which human effort cannot attain unless He relates men to a supernatural society and a new value-center. Christ is, indeed, a Christ of culture, but He is also a *Christ above culture*. This type is best represented by Thomas Aquinas and his followers.[4]

Converts in this category have never met a conference they didn't, or weren't tempted to, attend. They tend to be motivated by scholarly works. Much like a Western understanding of the study of theology, these converts make a science of the faith. Scholarship from seminaries and intellectual monastics become a never-ending thrill. It is almost a form of Gnosticism—hidden teachings—which call the convert and many a cradle, too, ever closer to the next book, seminar, or retreat.

Christ and Culture in Paradox

> In this group, the duality and inescapable authority of both Christ and culture is recognized, but the opposition between them is also accepted. Those falling into this category are Christians who are subject to the tension that accompanies obedience to two authorities who do not agree yet must both be obeyed. They are convicted that God requires obedience to the institutions of society and loyalty to its members as well as obedience to a Christ who sits in judgment on that society.

[4]Niebuhr, p. 42.

Hence man is seen as subject to two moralities, and as a citizen of two worlds that are not only discontinuous with each other but largely opposed. In the *polarity* and *tension* of Christ and culture life must be lived precariously and sinfully in the hope of a justification which lies beyond history. This type is best represented by Martin Luther.[5]

This is a frustrating category for converts, as it leaves room for grey areas, hence, inviting judgments from others. Converts may be used to "black" or "white" Christians, good guys and bad guys. Oddly, this model, best defined by Luther, can be a healthy one for some American Orthodox. That is, we live in a country not founded on Orthodox Christian monarchy or ideals. Though our heritage is inseparable from Judeo-Christian principles, nevertheless it is not an Orthodox culture (such as Russia, Greece, Romania, Serbia, or some areas of the Middle East).

Christ the Transformer of Culture

This final type is the *conversionist* solution to the problem. Those in this category understand with the members of the other four groups that human nature is fallen or perverted, and that this perversion not only appears in culture but is transmitted by it. Hence the opposition between Christ and all human institutions and customs is to be recognized. Yet the antithesis does not lead either to Christian separation from the world (as with *Christ against Culture*), or to mere endurance in the expectation of transhistoral salvation (as with *Christ and Culture in Paradox*). Christ is seen as the converter of man in his culture and society, not apart from these, for there is no nature without culture and no turning of men from self and idols to God save in society. Augustine is the chief proponent of this solution—also, John Calvin.[6]

The models of Tsarist Russia and ancient Byzantium come to mind. And any convert who worships in an "ethnic church" recognizes the above description and, it is to be hoped, has a better appreciation of his

[5]Niebuhr, pp. 42–43.
[6]Niebuhr, p. 43.

surrounding family. At one time, America would probably fit snugly within this paradigm—in traditional Protestantism.

But for all Orthodox, regardless of native culture, there is a paradigm missing from Neibuhr's list. That is the paradigm of *theosis*.[7]

Theosis

Theosis, or deification, comes through our cooperation with God. We must bring our will into submission to and union with the divine will to be saved. This is difficult, especially in light of the cultural paradigms listed above and the nature of our post-modern world.

If we struggle toward theosis with social and economic work, there are many difficulties all entangled with worldliness and mundane distractions. Within science or technology, the environment is in constant conflict with spiritual beliefs and needs. Harder still, thanks to fantastic and diabolical temptations, is the field of the arts. So how is it possible, given our culture, to be saved?

> Participation in culture is, from one point of view, a compromise so far as the spiritual life is concerned. Is not the method of deifying the world from within—the way which St Seraphim followed—a more sure course? Then everything else is transfigured as well.[8]

As St Seraphim said, "Find inner peace, and thousands around you will find salvation." If we are mindful of this personal struggle toward theosis, it is possible to be saved no matter what our cultural, familial, or societal circumstances.

---

[7]Theosis, or deification: "The grace of God through which believers grow to become like him and enjoy intimate communion with the Father through the Son in the Holy Spirit"; see *The Orthodox Study Bible* (Nashville: Thomas Nelson, 2008), p. 479.

[8]Elchaninov, p. 93.

16

Orthodox Evangelism

A small business owner once told of a guaranteed way to get rid of pesky phone sales people. "Whenever the salesman calls and immediately goes into his sales pitch," he said, "interrupt him with, 'Are you a born-again Christian?' If he replies 'No', you say, 'Well, I am and I don't deal with people who are not'—and hang up. If he replies 'Yes', you say, 'Well I'm not and don't deal with people who are'—and hang up. It works every time."

A couple years passed before I was quick enough to remember the story during one of those frequent dinnertime phone interruptions. As the pitch began, I said, "Are you a born-again Christian?" The stunned caller asked: "What am I supposed to say?" I said, "Just answer the question. Are you a born-again Christian?" "No," he replied. I said, "Well I am and I don't deal with folks who aren't!" I hung up. Forgive me, but my wife and I had a good laugh. Before the chuckles faded the phone rang again. "Hello?" The voice on the other end shouted, "I am! I am! I am!" (Ha! Talk about a short catechumenate!)

"How *do* the Orthodox evangelize?" The question was posed by a visiting Methodist pastor. It wasn't a question I was used to answering. I was stumped. My sinister side wanted to blurt out: "Not very well!" But this is not true. With hosts of Evangelicals, Episcopalians, and others coming home to holy Orthodoxy, something evangelical is going on. Honestly, other than poorly, I don't remember how I answered the question.

The fact that we live in a culture that is still fairly familiar with Jesus Christ should not prevent us from humbly and boldly imparting the fundamentals of the faith, over and over again, even to the faithful Christians around us. The fundamentals, the basics, mere Christianity—this is what our society thirsts for, this living water. The popular social knowledge of our Lord has become something other than truth. Jesus is made out to be a mere buddy or pal who is there in our times of trouble, like an insurance company. We who share in the fullness of the faith are *bound* to share this treasure with those around us. Along the way, as you will see below, there's ample opportunity for error and missed opportunities.

An Orthodox Christian friend of mine was constantly bothered by Protestant and sectarian missionaries in his suburban apartment. One evening he decided to have a bit of fun. Two young men were fervently trying to entice him with the glories of "guaranteed salvation." He took them on a tour of his home. He introduced them to all the icons populating his walls. When he got to an icon of the Theotokos holding Christ, he said, "This is Mary and . . . uh . . . Mary and . . . oh, gosh . . . uh." One of the Bible thumpers dubiously gasped, "Jesus?" "YES! That's it! Jesus!" he replied. They made a hasty and lasting exit.

There used to be a Baptist minister in my town with the same name as me. On occasion, we'd gotten each other's phone calls. One evening an Orthodox Christian called long distance from a pay phone. He reached the "Rev. Huneycutt" instead of "Fr Joseph." He decided, what the heck, to have a conversation with the preacher. Eventually the minister started asking questions about Orthodoxy. True to form, he finally asked my friend, "Do you know the Lord?" The caller replied, "Yes, I know the Lord, his Father, and his Mother!" This is where the conversation broke down.

There is much work to be done if we are to introduce true Christianity into this wayward society. Yet if we're too full of zeal to convert our neighbor, chances are we've neglected God in the process. Christ said, "Love God. Love your neighbor." Some have interpreted this to mean, "Convert your neighbor and God will love you." We must begin with God's love and love of God. Before we do anything else, we must love God above all. Salvation is the Good News of God's love that has consumed our very being. This consummation is the beginning of salvation. We must bring our will into accord with God's in order to be a Christian and bear Christ to the world. The Theotokos is our model for this fundamental step.[1]

While I was working in a local hospital some years ago, a man approached me and wanted to pray. Afterwards, he began speaking of his faith and I listened and wondered where this was all leading. I soon figured out that he thought I was a Roman Catholic and he was intent on converting me to Jesus Christ. After I told him about Orthodoxy, he was much more interested in me as a fellow Christian. He even wanted to know the location of the church. Thinking I'd won this little faith skirmish, I smiled, gave him my card, shook his hand, and turned to leave. "You don't pray to Mary, do you?" he asked. Whoa! "What?" I pretended. "Y'all don't pray to Mary, do you?"

What to say? Knowing of his bias I asked, "You mean like the Roman Catholics do?" "Yes," he replied. "No," said this silly Orthodox priest. Okay, okay, I realize I blew it. But listen to what comes next. He smiled and said, "Good, because Mary scares the Hell out of me!" I was tested. I failed.

I once stood outside a hospital elevator, dressed in my cassock, with the Sacrament hanging around my neck. I was there to give Communion to an Orthodox Christian. A young woman approached the elevator, burst out laughing, and asked: "What are you?" Caught off guard, I replied, "I'm an Orthodox priest. What, may I ask, are you?" "Well, I'm Baptist," she boasted. "Good," I said as we entered the elevator. On the way up she said, "We believe in Jesus Christ." "That's good," I stammered, "we do too." "Huh! I thought y'all believed in Mother Mary," she snorted. "Yes, we believe in the Lord's Mother as well. . . ." Before I could continue she announced:

---

[1]"For two thousand years the Church has preserved the memory of the Virgin Mary as the prototype of all Christians—the model of what we are to become in Christ. Mary was truly pure and unconditionally obedient to God. The tradition of the Church holds that Mary remained a virgin all her life. While lifelong celibacy is not a model for all Christians to follow, Mary's spiritual purity, her wholehearted devotion to God, is certainly to be emulated.

Mary is also our model in that she was the first person to receive Jesus Christ. As Mary bore Christ in her womb physically, all Christians now have the privilege of bearing God within them spiritually. By God's grace and mercy we are purified and empowered to become like Him." *The Orthodox Study Bible: New Testament and Psalms* (Nashville: Thomas Nelson, 1993), p. 135.

"We put our faith only in the blood of Jesus!" Without even thinking I caressed the tabernacle and said, "That's exactly what I have right here." Just then the elevator doors sprang open, as did her mouth, and she virtually ran out of the elevator down the hall. End of discussion.

I believe we fail sometimes because we fear we lack the right answers. We also fear rejection. No one likes to be rejected. Yet, Christ's disciples should expect to be rejected and even hated:

> If the world hates you, know that it has hated me before it hated you. If you were of the world, the world would love its own; but because you are not of the world, but I chose you out of the world, therefore the world hates you. If they persecuted me, they will persecute you (Jn 15.18–19, 20b).

When we run from rejection, hatred, scorn and derision, we are no different from the disciples who fled the scene when it included crucifixion. But they changed. They were converted. Unlike the disciples at the time, we have the benefit of knowing the rest of the story: the resurrection. What else could have happened to change these scared and hurting men into the great evangelists and martyrs of the faith? They experienced the resurrection. This, the greatest revelation of God, changed them. They converted. Death no longer held sway—not only over their bodies, but over their fears. They began to die to themselves to live a greater life in Christ.

We, too, must convert—be willing to die for the faith—before we can evangelize. Now you might say, "Gee, that sounds a bit extreme." I agree with you. But the faith is not something that we make up. The faith is not something that necessarily soothes us. The faith is a precious gift from God that requires *all* of us: mind, body, and soul. We may have to die many "little deaths" before the big one that terminates our earthly sojourn. For now, Christ calls us out of the world. He consumes us, and sends us back with fear of God and full of the Holy Spirit to bring in the harvest. We must die for him to live in us. We must allow our pride to die, our greed to die, our wants to die, our wills to die, our dreams to die, our feelings to die. *We must die.* Death is the first step in evangelism.

Like St John the Forerunner, we must say of Christ: "He must increase, but I must decrease" (Jn 3.30). In taking up our cross daily we crucify our sinful selves only to be raised up to glory and thereby become co-workers with God for the salvation of the world. This is the promise. This is the mission. Evangelism begins with death. We are not to slay our brother for the sake of the gospel. Rather, we must be slain. This is the way of evangelism.

In conjunction with the first step is the second: prayer. We must spend time with God. Sure, God is everywhere and available always. But we are not. Our busy lives usually serve up schedules where we know not whether we're coming or going. We need to spend time just plain standing: standing in the presence of God in prayer. This presence with God is incarnational, involving the sacraments of the Church. It also entails time alone, or with family, in our icon corners.

The next step in evangelism is *social*. We have to be around other people in order to bring them the good news. This, being in contact with people, happens each and every day in ordinary ways. The day's fleeting moments are often unrecognized as evangelism's finest hour.

Back when I was just starting out as a missionary priest, an experienced priest told me: "Pray God sends you people. Pray you recognize the people God sends you." Living this principle is difficult. Oftentimes one can feel the responsibility for "converting" everyone who smiles toward Orthodoxy. We get our hopes up when a new face darkens the church door. Too many times we allow ourselves to count un-hatched chickens. This can lead to mental and emotional exhaustion.

We must be present with God and present with others. The operative word here is *present*. If we're not living in the present, we're not residing in God. We wrongly reject what the French mystic, Jean Pierre de Caussade, calls *the sacrament of the present moment*.[2] This "sacrament" is offered by God with each moment. Yet most of the time, we reside not in that moment, but in the past or future—the land of worry, doubt, fear, and concern. This is not to say that most of us have never tasted this precious

---

[2]Jean-Pierre de Caussade, *The Sacrament of the Present Moment* (reissue edition: San Francisco: HarperSanFrancisco, 2009).

sacrament of God's grace. We have. However, this joy is often quickly discarded only to be replaced by *our* will: future, past, pride, sloth, worry.

This *moment* that God offers us is not an individual right. It involves personal relationships. It begs us to be the "God bearer" to the world around us. It begs us to recognize Christ in others. Living in the present necessitates love and forgiveness. For there is no other way for us to reside in the will of God than to be living, loving, and forgiving in the present moment. We evangelize by:

1) dying to self

2) being present with God

3) being present with others

If we do these things we fulfill the commandments of Christ to love God and our neighbor. This sounds simple. It is simple. God is simple. For fallen humans, it is terribly hard. It is much easier to spout doctrine, judge our neighbors, be puffed up with pride—and hide.

Orthodox evangelism is not a matter of endless programs, workshops, revivals, audio and video tapes, etc. Like training wheels, these can be helpful, but they are not the best means. Christ said there is one thing needful. This one thing needful, the inner peace—Christ—leads us to act. The Apostle Paul wrote to Timothy:

> I charge you therefore before God and the Lord Jesus Christ, who will judge the living and the dead at His appearing and His kingdom: Preach the word! Be ready in season and out of season. Convince, rebuke, exhort, with all longsuffering and teaching.
>
> For the time will come when they will not endure sound doctrine, but according to their own desires, because they have itching ears, they will heap up for themselves teachers; and they will turn their ears away from the truth, and be turned aside by fables.
>
> But you be watchful in all things, endure afflictions, do the work of an evangelist, fulfill your ministry (2 Tim 4.1–5).[3]

---

[3]Taken from the New King James Version.

God forbid that we Orthodox un-shoulder the burden that God has placed on us. Rejection of our calling is a rejection of the kingdom. We have a calling to share this precious faith with the world for its salvation. This salvation was purchased by the blood of the Lamb. This faith has sprung from the blood of the martyrs and the prayers of the saints. Against this faith, this Church, the gates of Hell shall not prevail. We are the people of God; the time is now. Let us work out our own salvation with fear and trembling. Let us struggle to die to self and to be found in the presence of God and others.

The decisive step in evangelism is trust. In dying to self, being present with God and others, we trust. We trust that through our imperfect and unworthy efforts, God will bless the increase and the Holy Spirit will lead others into the Church.

17

Concerning the Clergy

Some time or another, many converts will be forced to conclude that it is not the individual bishop or priest, but the faith—the Church—that saves them. As stated earlier, zeal often wanes; this, coupled with the fact that the bishop and priest have clay feet, may often lead to a cold and sobering reality for the newbie. Our faith is not in a man, but in the God-Man, Christ. The God-established hierarchy of the Church is answerable to him. We have only one task: be faithful!

Much like the charismatic preacher in Protestant communities, the priest can be a definite "draw." The traditional street attire, vestments, and outward appearance may create a mystique of other-worldliness, holiness, in the eyes of the convert. Great! But the holiness is God's. There will come a time when the convert discovers that the bishop or priest is a man. He's a man with strengths, weaknesses, shortcomings, and the like. He makes mistakes. And, unlike the ways of the world, the God-pleasing shepherd is not permitted to reveal *all* to those with itching ears.

Back when I was an adolescent, thinking myself a chosen man of God, I had a disagreement with my Southern Baptist minister. It was the 70s. I was a teen. He was a square. But that's not the reason. The problem revolved around another cooler, hipper, preacher. The latter we'll refer to as "Reverend Green."

Though he didn't pastor a church, Reverend Green was a dynamic evangelist. I'd heard him preach a couple times at youth rallies, prayer breakfasts and such. Boy, was he ever on fire! Green really held my attention and I thought: "Cool! I want him to be my preacher!" He had a gift. He was vibrant and on fire for the Lord. He was the man!

During a youth meeting I suggested inviting him to preach at our church. The others agreed and our request was submitted to the pastor. You guessed it. The answer was "No." Fuddy Duddy! We didn't understand and, as it turns out, the pastor wouldn't give us teens the real reasons. It got to the point where we, I should say *I*, demanded a meeting. He heard me out; still, he refused. He wasn't cool. He just didn't understand. He was . . . *Arrgh!* I thought, "He's got to go." If memory serves, I believe I even sent him a letter asking him to do just that: *leave.*

Years later I learned that the happ'nin pastor was happ'nin in places he shouldn't have been. You are correct, dear reader. He ran off with a church secretary, another man's wife. Or was it the organist? I can't remember. But I remember the lesson; that is, we ought not make a habit of throwing stones at clergy because, often, we don't know the whole story. The pastor may not even have all the details; and it's very likely that he wouldn't—couldn't—tell them if he did.

It is the same in Orthodoxy, even more so. Many times, the priest or bishop is unable to be totally forthcoming about certain matters because they are confidential and/or would cause greater scandal if all was told.

Over the years I've come to have profound respect for clergy who can keep their mouth shut and carry on serving God and Man with love and joy. Believe me, it would be much easier to become resentful, bitter, and mean. Even worse, the priest could become an old gossip, letting junk just fall out of his mouth with ease. The temptations are always there.

One priest told me told me of his inaugural conversation with his bishop wherein he expressed interest in ordination. The crusty old man looked him straight in the eye and said, "Boy, do you pray?"

"Why yes, I pray every day . . ."

"Pray to God you don't have this curse!" said the bishop.

I think the old man had let the vocation get the better of him. It happens. Or, as one priest said: "I wanted to be a priest out of arrogance; God allows me to be one as a penance."

Once, at a Diocesan Convention in Atlanta, Bishop Basil (Essey) delivered a homily about priests—not just any priests, but the ones that were seated right in front of His Grace and 2,000 worshipers. He talked of their struggles, their crosses, sacrifices they—and their families—make to serve. He encouraged the faithful to pray for their priest and to lovingly support him and his family. I was a "baby priest" at the time and couldn't fully appreciate or understand why so many of the men around me were weeping. Sobbing priests; crying their eyes out. I know now.

I no longer judge fellow priests, or any pastor, as harshly as I used to. This is not to suggest that I always agree with them, like their practices, or even like them. But being hardheaded and a slow learner, I think my temperance (what little there is of it, and God knows I need it) is a direct result of my own battle scars. Trust me, a man who has served the Lord's altar for many years has seen, heard, and experienced just about every temptation Satan can come up with. They, the elder clergy, inspire me.

Don't misunderstand me; there are bad apples (e.g., the above illustration and all those "situations" the media loves to report). I've met a few in the Orthodox Church. But the sacrificial nature of the vocation has a way of purging and honing even the roughest of edges. By and large, parishioners are patient and God is merciful.

The pastor's real struggle, as with everyone, is the day-to-day struggle of sin and salvation. For the pastor, this means not only his own salvation and that of his family, but also that of his flock. You think you have sleepless nights, worrying about your children? So does the pastor, worrying about his flock.

Do your children break your heart by the things they say and do? *Pastor, flock.*

Do you pray for your children, weep over them when they're not looking? *Pastor, flock.*

Do you sometimes look at your children and think, "Huh?" *Pastor, flock.*

Do your children sometimes give you dirty looks when you correct them? *Pastor, flock.*

No matter how many times they break your heart are you there for them? *Pastor, flock.*

Do you know things about yourself and other people that you don't share with your children, in order preserve their innocence as long as you can, and not be a temptation to them? *Pastor, flock.*

Do you know things about your children that you refuse to reveal? *Pastor, flock.*

Most of all, do you love and delight in your children? *Pastor, flock.*

Over the years I've been shocked when clergy actually *do* divulge stuff. I'm not talking about things heard in confession, God forbid! Rather, scandal eventually hits all parishes and the priest tries mightily to protect his children, the flock. But often are the times when folks try to put a self-helping spin on their failings. Mixing in a good bit of sin can tempt one to find someone, anyone, to blame. Like, for instance, the priest! That's it! The priest is to blame!

Sometimes he is.

Most times—most priests—are not.

I once had a well-loved parishioner suddenly quit the parish. There were a few who thought, "Father ran him off!" Such talk usually dies down as the grieving process proceeds, but this went on for some time. Having divulged the true reason for the man's departure (truly scandalous) to the bishop, he said, "If it's affecting someone's salvation and they just won't stop talking about it –tell them." And I did. It helped, thank God. But those times have been few. Mature Christians know better. Oftentimes they know better than the priest and help to remind him that "God prunes his Church."

After a while, the priest gets used to it. He never likes it. He suffers for it. But he reaches an understanding with himself that, for sanity's sake, and that of his family and his flock, he's just going to keep struggling toward the Kingdom as best he's able.

At a candid clergy gathering, where the topic was "Antagonists in the Church," an experienced priest told of an early trial in his ministry. Someone in his parish had started a rumor about his wife. It became a scandal. Like all such devilry, it snowballed. At one point the wife asked her husband:

Why? Why keep on? Why not leave and go to another parish? Why not give up the nonsense and get a "real job?"

The priest, with tears in his eyes, told the rest of us what he had told his wife, "Honey, you don't understand. I get to stand at the altar of the Most High and touch the precious body of our Lord at every liturgy."

We all understood.

Standing before the altar, celebrating the mysteries of the Church, is an experience incomparable to any this side of the grave. No man should ever take it lightly. Few are they who remain unchanged by this awesome and sacred duty. For lack of better wording, it makes it all worth it.

Our imperfect world—outside paradise, ruled by the enemy—has taught us to question all authority, and has denigrated fatherhood. But as Christians, we know that all fatherhood flows from the Father. It is his Fatherhood that should be the model, the ideal, for earthly fathers. We should not judge fatherhood according to the ways of the world. Rather, the changeless Fatherhood of God is known through the Church. St Cyprian of Carthage wrote: "No one can have God as Father who does not have the Church as Mother."

And somewhere along the line, God willing, we children all fit in.

Most of the time your priest is just a man struggling toward salvation, bowed a little lower each year with the weight of his sins, the burden of "parenting," and the glory of the cross. Standing at the altar, it's all worth it. All of it. Worth it.

Pray for your pastor. (Even if he is a square.)

18

The Good in Priesthood

"Okay, you've told us about the 'bad' regarding the priesthood. There's something 'good' about being a priest, right? What's good about the priesthood?" This query came from a convert wife, married to a revert who was flirting with a vocation. What did I say? I laughed. I had no answer. I later asked the question of several colleagues. They howled. What's the "good" in priesthood?

"More stormy billows vex the soul of the priest than the gales which disturb the sea."[1]

It is difficult to speak of the "good" in priesthood chiefly because a "good" is something we normally take pride in. Yet, pride is the sin that wipes away humility, which is the very ministry to which priests are called. One thing must be said at the outset, by "good" we are not referring to "happy." In other words, this *good* is not an emotion or a possession. For most, the priesthood will not provide earthly riches.

However, as with any vocation or profession, the priesthood does provide happy moments. There are plenty of parties and celebrations, births, weddings, and social events included within the life of a priest. Yet the *good* in the priesthood may not resemble the *happy* things of life in the least. For a *good* is often something we glory in. "But far be it from me to glory except in the cross of our Lord Jesus Christ, through whom the world has been crucified to me and I to the world," writes St Paul to the Galatians (6.14).

---

[1] St John Chrysostom, "On the Priesthood," *Nicene and Post-Nicene Fathers of the Christian Church*, First Series [NPNF¹], Vol. 9 (Grand Rapids: Eerdmans, c. 1975), p. 49.

Trying to grasp the *good* in priesthood, using the common worldly understanding of *good*, is like trying to hold onto smoke. Perhaps this is because our view of what is good and our experiences of the priesthood seemingly have little in common. Why is this? Maybe God's definition of good differs from ours? This is certainly the case.

I believe that unless one is called by the providence of God to the holy priesthood, he will fail. Fr Alexander Schmemann wrote:

> No one can take it upon himself to become a priest, to decide on the basis of his own qualifications, preparation and predispositions. The vocation always comes from above—from God's *ordination and order. It is not 'priesthood' that the priest receives in his ordination, but the gift of Christ's love, that love which made Christ the only priest and which fills with this unique priesthood, the ministry of those whom He sends to His people.*[2]

Obedience to the call from God is inherently good. The Theotokos is our model in this call of obedience. By saying "yes" to God she bore the Salvation of the world, which is Christ. In the same manner, a priest is called to be a type of God-bearer by his obedience. Then again, what was prophesied of Mary can be said of priests: "a sword will pierce through your own soul also."

St Gregory of Nazianzus teaches us:

> We have, against the fear of office, a possible help in the law of obedience, inasmuch as God in His goodness rewards our faith, and makes a perfect ruler of the man who has confidence in Him, and places all his hopes in Him; but against the danger of disobedience I know of nothing which can help us, and of no ground to encourage our confidence.[3]

Obedience is intrinsically good. If a priest is obedient to the will of God, that constitutes a good. Without this good any fruit borne of his ministry

---

[2]Fr Alexander Schmemann, *For the Life of the World* (Crestwood, NY: St Vladimir's Seminary Press, 1963), p. 94.

[3]St Gregory Nazianzus, *Oration* 2.113 (NPNF[2] 7:226).

will be dark and bitter. Soon the disobedient priest will be but a barren and withered fig tree (Mk 11.20–26). Such is not the will and call of God.

Perhaps therefore we laugh without a ready answer to the question, "What's good about the priesthood?" We laugh because, the truth is, we know all the wrong answers to the question. There is nothing inherently good in *just* being a priest. God forbid that we should teach our children, female and male, that the very highest way to serve God is by being up front, in some "official" capacity. If we do, we educate them in a falsehood.

Sacrifice is the essence of the priesthood. The priesthood of all believers (laity and clergy) is filled with sacrifice. We betray this truth when we view participation around the altar, behind the iconostasis—*up front*—as somehow superior to the indispensable ministry of the gathered faithful as the sacrificing community of God.

Once a man has *obeyed* the call for ordination, he will soon become acquainted with the essence of the priestly ministry: sacrifice. How can sacrifice be seen as good? The same way "Good Friday" is good! That is, in sacrificing himself for others, the priest models him whom he represents. Sacrificing is life giving. The devil, often disguised as an angel of light, refuses to sacrifice. Self-indulgence, not sacrificing, leads to death. Sacrifice differentiates good from evil. Sacrifice is inherently good. God-pleasing sacrifice is to be offered on behalf of all and for all to the Triune God and Creator of all. Gregory of Nazianzus writes of the priest:

> For he seeks not his own interests, but those of his children, whom he has begotten in Christ by the gospel. This is the aim of all his spiritual authority, in everything to neglect his own in comparison with the advantage of others.[4]

When, in St Matthew's Gospel, the rich young ruler approaches Christ and asks how to inherit eternal life, the query is prefaced by the salutation "Good Teacher." "Why do you call Me good?" replies Christ, "No one is good but One, that is, God" (Mt 19.16–23). Herein lies the answer to our question. What is good about the priesthood? God. The immeasurable joy

[4]St Gregory Nazianzus, *Oration* 2.54 (NPNF[2] 7:216).

that one experiences when he and others are drawn into the never-ending Mystery, which is God, is truly the *good* that fuels one's priestly ministry.

The faith of the priest is continually enhanced by the faith of the flock. This faith understands its creator as a God of mercy, compassion, and love for mankind. God works through people and our experience of this, sinful though we are, is a good that passes human understanding. The sacrificing priest reveals God to his flock and reconciles the people to God. This is the ministry of Christ that is made manifest in his priests. For it is not our ministry but God's. It is not our priesthood, but Christ's. George Florovsky says of priests:

> They are acting primarily in *persona Christi*. They are representatives of Christ himself, not of believers; and in them and through them the head of the Body, the only High Priest of the New Covenant, is preforming, continuing and accomplishing his eternal pastoral and priestly office. He is himself the only true minister of the Church.[5]

This ministry of obedience, sacrifice, revelation, and reconciliation is improbable—nay impossible—without a special grace from God. Before a man can serve in the priestly office, he must be given a special *charism*, or gift, from the Holy Spirit. This gift—the grace of the priesthood—is necessary for any and all *good* to come from this sacred ministry. During the ordination rite, the bishops prays:

> O God great in might and inscrutable in wisdom, marvelous in counsel above the sons of men: Do thou, the same Lord, fill with the gift of the Holy Spirit this man whom it hath pleased thee to advance to the degree of priest; that he may be worthy to stand in innocency before thine Altar; to proclaim the Gospel of thy kingdom; to minister the word of thy truth; to offer unto thee spiritual gifts and sacrifices; to renew thy people through the laver of regeneration. That when he shall go to meet thee, at the Second Coming of our great God and Savior, Jesus Christ, thine Only-begotten Son, he may receive the reward of

---

[5] Archpriest George Florovsky, *On the Catholicity of the Church.* http://www.fatheralexander.org/booklets/english/catholicity_church_florovsky.htm (accessed August 11, 2017).

a good steward in the degree committed unto him through the pleni-
tude of thy goodness.[6]

The Holy Spirit is invoked upon the candidate in order for him to
proclaim the gospel, minister the word of truth, offer spiritual gifts and
sacrifices, and to renew the people of God. Then, and only then, are the
true good things of God bestowed upon him—and that at the Last Day!
Yet, the *good* that is found in between this life and the next is in being
obedient to the call and charism. It is the struggle, the spiritual warfare,
the unceasing love of God, and the promise of his kingdom that are the
good things this side of the grave. Without any of these, we have only
Satan, sin, and death.

In obedience to God, the priest leads his flock toward their eternal
reward with the Triune God. Again, St Gregory writes:

> But the scope of our art is to provide the soul with wings, to rescue it
> from the world and give it to God, and to watch over that which is in
> His image, if it abides, to take it by the hand, if it is in danger, to restore
> it, if ruined, to make Christ to dwell in the heart by the Spirit; and, in
> short, to deify, and bestow heavenly bliss upon, one who belongs to
> the heavenly host.[7]

The *good* in the priesthood is the priesthood of Christ. The good in
the priesthood is the "already and not yet" of the kingdom of God. The
priest re-presents the great High Priest, Jesus Christ, who is the ultimate
sacrifice for the sake of the world and its salvation. This same Christ, who
is God, is *the Good* of the priesthood. The priest must be ever mindful of
this in order to faithfully serve his ministry in Christ.

However, in the process of re-presenting and sacrificing, the priest will
experience his own pain and suffering on behalf of all and for all to the
glory of God.

---

[6]*Service Book of the Holy Eastern Orthodox Catholic and Apostolic Church according to
the use of the Antiochian Orthodox Christian Archdiocese of North America* (Ninth Edition,
1993), pp. 234–235.
[7]St Gregory Nazianzus, *Oration* 2.22 (NPNF[2] 7:209).

The pastor therefore ought to be of noble spirit, so as not to despond, or to despair of the salvation of the wanderers from the fold, but continually reason with himself and say, "Perhaps God will give them repentance to the acknowledging of the truth, and that they may recover themselves out of the snare of the devil"[8]

Thus, the priest ought to be protected on all sides by a kind of adamantine armor, by intense earnestness, and perpetual watchfulness concerning his manner of life, lest someone discovering an exposed and neglected spot should inflict a deadly wound: for all who surround him are ready to smite and overthrow him: not enemies only and adversaries, but many even of those who profess friendship.[9]

What is good in this? *Salvation.* In the struggle of spiritual warfare, both within the priest and among his flock, the good fight is fought amid pain and suffering with the constant remembrance that God is with us. God's presence does not always feel warm and fuzzy. Sometimes God is presented on the cross. Sometimes the priest is made the "sacrificial lamb" by his peers, or even his own flock. At other times, the weight of suffering, both his own and that of the flock, hones his ministry. This *good* leads to compassion.

It is quite dizzying for the modern, materialistic, secularist mind to comprehend suffering as a good. Yet if we read church history and the lives of the saints, we see that suffering is necessary for salvation in much the same way that death is necessary for resurrection and life eternal. This is the ministry of the Compassionate One, who leads us toward compassion.

Compassion is the good fruit born of a faithful ministry to God and his people. This ministry begs us to recognize Christ in others. As God is compassionate, so are we to be. The priestly ministry is permeated with love and forgiveness. For there is no other way for us to reside in the will of God than to be living, loving, and forgiving. We either come by this

---

[8]Chrysostom, *Six Books on the Priesthood* 2 (NPNF[1] 9:41–42).
[9]Chrysostom, *Six Books on the Priesthood* 3 (NPNF[1] 9:52).

willingly—or through hard knocks. Either way, it is the will of God and will be done, often in spite of ourselves.

The glory of the priesthood is the glory of the cross. The *good* in priesthood does not belong to the priest nor to this earth. What is good about the priesthood is the recurring insight, provided by God's grace, that one is doing the will of God. The good of the priesthood is in continually realizing that God is good. The good of the priesthood is in sharing the goodness of God, even his precious body and blood, with others who, along with the priest, are unworthy of this great good. "No one is good but One, that is, God." St Gregory of Nazianzus states:

> Yesterday I was crucified with Him; today I am glorified with Him, yesterday I died with Him; today I am quickened with Him; yesterday I was buried with Him; today I rise with Him. But let us offer to Him Who suffered and rose again for us [ourselves] . . . the possession most precious to God, and most fitting; let us give back to the Image what is made after the Image. . . . Let us give all, offer all, to Him Who gave Himself a Ransom and a Reconciliation for us.[10]

Thus, the glory that is to come fortifies the present ministry of the sacrificing priest. This is not only good, but necessary for his salvation. Over and over again, the question arises, "What's good in the priesthood?" The answer is, in a word, Christ. For in this ministry, over and over again, we recognize that apart from him we can do nothing. If priests are faithful in imparting this wisdom to those in their charge, they shall receive the reward of a *good* steward at the second coming of our great God and Savior, Jesus Christ.

---

[10]St Gregory Nazianzus, *Oration* 1.4–5 (NPNF[1] 7:203).

19

A Final Word

There is no universally defining characteristic of American Orthodoxy. It is easy to label folks, pigeonholing them into a category. I have even employed the device throughout this book—convert, cradle, revert, retread. But you know what? All are Orthodox. We are all family.

One of my personal joys—as husband, father, and priest—is family prayer. The Huneycutts struggle to pray as a family every night. As this book goes to press,[1] the three-year-old, Helen, starts us out with "In the Name of the Father . . . and of the Son . . . and of the Holy Spirit. Amen." Then the seven-year-old, Basil, does his part of our family ritual, leading us through the introductory prayers, the Trisagion. Daddy does the benediction at the end of the Our Father. Here's where our prayer pro, eleven-year-old Mary Catherine, takes over. She prays selections from Evening Prayers as she has been doing since she was four.

Our time concludes with a reading from the lives of the saints. This is one of my favorite parts of the day: hearing about the heroes and heroines of the faith. The kids like it, too. Sometimes during our prayers, for some reason, my wife and I look over at each other and, without words, smile and wonder at the mystery and blessing of parenting. What a joy. I am unworthy.

Before all five of us are the icons adorning our family icon corner: The Life Giving Spring (Christ and his Mother), St Joseph the Betrothed, St Elizabeth (Mother of the Forerunner), St Andrew the First-Called, St Mary Magdalene, St Basil of Kineshma, Sts Constantine and Helen, and St Raphael of Brooklyn.

---

[1] The first edition of this book went to press in 2006.—*Ed.*

Each night, standing in prayer, I can't help but notice our children's growth: physically, mentally, and spiritually. It's a wonder to behold. There are not many things that I do each day that I look back on with total contentment. Yet, family prayer fits that bill. I'm not always motivated, fully alert, or even willing. But I always leave changed, blessed; different.

I'm helped in this transition by my family with me—Elizabeth, Mary, Basil, and Helen—and my family before me: Christ and his Mother, St Joseph, St Elizabeth, St Andrew, St Mary Magdalene, St Basil of Kineshma, Sts Constantine and Helen, and St Raphael of Brooklyn.

For those families who are Orthodox, I commend the practice of saying prayers each night, gathered as family. I hope that, for the non-Orthodox, the above sketch sheds light on a rather peculiar space in most Orthodox homes, the home altar or icon corner. I also see another image. I can only imagine how God the Father looks upon us, his children. He sees our growth physically, mentally, spiritually. I can only imagine that it is a wonder to behold.

He sees us differently, of course. God judges our heart rather than our ethnicity, religious pedigree, culture, kookiness, or station in life. There won't be any jurisdictions in heaven. There'll be nothing but converts—those who continually convert to be like children to enter the Kingdom.

An old and successful parishioner once told me: "One of the keys to successful living is being able to adapt to the changes." Change is inevitable. Yet just as "Christ is the same yesterday, today, and forever" (Heb 13.8)—so shall the Church be. A rudimentary study of Byzantine history reveals many changes wrought by fallible humans throughout that era in the Church. Yet the same Church now being found by American converts, reverts, and retreads—founded by Christ upon the Apostles—is the same Ark of Salvation that found our Byzantine brethren within her embrace many years ago. It is the same faith being experienced anew in Russia. It will endure throughout all time. For now, its witness is a fledgling mission in America. Should the Lord tarry, there will inevitably develop an "American expression" of the true faith in a land populated with immigrants from many nations. In the meantime we may all look a bit crazy, flying over, while praying within, that onion dome. *Glory to God for all things!*

Appendix

Apostolic Canon 31

If any Presbyter, condemning his own bishop, draw people aside and set up another altar, without finding anything wrong with the bishop in point of piety and righteousness, let him be deposed, on the ground that he is an office-seeker. For he is a tyrant. Let the rest of clergymen be treated likewise, and all those who abet him. But let the laymen be excommunicated. Let these things be done after one, and a second, and a third request of the bishop.

Interpretation (of Sts Nikodemos and Agapios):

Order sustains the coherence of both heavenly things and earthly things, according to St Gregory the Theologian. So good order ought to be kept everywhere as helping coherence and preserving the established system, and especially among ecclesiastics, who need to know their own standards, and to avoid exceeding the limits and bounds of their own class. But as for Presbyters, and Deacons, and all clergymen they ought to submit to their own bishop; the bishops, in turn, to their own Metropolitan; the Metropolitans, to their own Patriarch. On this account the present Apostolical Canon ordains as follows: Any presbyter that scorns his own bishop, and without knowing that the latter is manifestly at fault either in point of piety or in point of righteousness—that is to say, without knowing him to be manifestly either heretical or unjust—proceeds to gather the Christians into a distinct group and to build another church, and should hold services separately, without the permission and approval of his bishop in so doing, on the ground of his being an office-seeker he is to be deposed; since like a tyrant with violence and tyranny he is trying to wrest away the authority which belongs to his bishop. But also any other clergymen that agree with him in such apostasy must be deposed from office too just as he must; but as for those who are laymen, let them be excommunicated. These things, however, are to be done after the bishop three times gently and blandly urges those who have separated from him to forgo such a movement, and they obstinately refuse to do so.

Ss Nicodemus and Apapius (eds.), *The Rudder,*
trans. D. Cummings (New York: Luna Printing, 1983), p.46.

Atonement: ("at-one-ment")

Man's reconciliation with God through the sacrificial death of Christ.

In the 11th–12th centuries, with Anselm's *Cur Deus Homo,* the emphasis shifted. The role of Satan receded and its place was taken by the idea of satisfaction. Sin, being an infinite offence against God, required a satisfaction equally infinite. As no finite being, man or angel, could offer such satisfaction, it was necessary that an infinite being, viz. God Himself, should take the place of man and, by His death, make complete satisfaction to Divine Justice. Hence the death of Christ was not a ransom paid to the devil but a debt paid to the Father.

The Oxford Dictionary of the Christian Church [ODCC]
(Oxford University Press, 1983), p.104.

Council of Florence (1438–1445)

Its chief object was reunion with the Greek Church, which sought support from the West against the Turks, who were nearing Constantinople. Statements on the Eucharist and on papal primacy, which caused some difficulty, on Purgatory and on the legitimacy of the Filioque clause were presented and eventually accepted. These were incorporated into the Decree of Union . . . which was eventually signed on 5 July 1439 and solemnly promulgated the following day. Mark of Ephesus was the only bishop to refuse his signature. The union was challenged by popular sentiment and later rejected by the Orthodox.

ODCC, pp. 518–519.

Filioque

(Latin: "And the Son") The dogmatic formula expressing the Double Procession of the Holy Spirit, added by the Western Church to the Nicene-Constantinopolitan Creed. . . . It was no part of the original Creed. . . . Since the time of Photius, who violently denounced it, the "Filioque" has been made the chief ground of attack by the Orthodox Church on the Church of Rome.

> *The Oxford Dictionary of the Christian Church*, 3rd ed., F. L. Cross and E. A. Livingstone, eds. (Oxford: Oxford University Press, 2005), 614.

Manichaeism

Manes, the founder of Manichaeism . . . transformed the cramped, ritualist views of the Judeo-Christian sect in which he had been brought up into a coherent body of Gnostic dogma, uncompromisingly dualistic, consequential, and deeply conscious of having "unveiled" truths of universal validity. It was based on a supposed primeval conflict between light and darkness. It taught that the object of the practice of religion was to release the particles of light which Satan had stolen from the world of Light and imprisoned in man's brain and that Jesus, Buddha, the Prophets, and Manes had been sent to help in this task. For the Manichaean believer, the whole physical universe was mobilized to create this release. The Gnostic myth of salvation has seldom been presented on so grandiose a cosmic scale, worked out in rigorous detail; every phase of the movements of the sun, moon and stars was a stage in the deliverance of the believer's soul, and every ritual act of the individual had resonance among the heavenly bodies.

> *ODCC*, p.864.

Nicene-Constantinopolitan Creed
(also called the Nicene Creed, the Symbol of Faith, or simply the Creed):

We[1] believe in one God, the Father Almighty, Maker of heaven and earth, and of all things visible and invisible;

And in one Lord, Jesus Christ, the Son of God, the Only-begotten, Begotten of the Father before all ages, Light of Light, true God of true God, Begotten, not made, of one essence with the Father, by whom all things were made:

Who for us men and for our salvation came down from heaven, and was incarnate of the Holy Spirit and the Virgin Mary, and was made man;

And was crucified also for us under Pontius Pilate, and suffered and was buried;

And the third day He rose again, according to the Scriptures;

And ascended into heaven, and sitteth at the right hand of the Father;

And he shall come again with glory to judge the living and the dead, whose kingdom shall have no end.

And we believe in the Holy Spirit, the Lord, and Giver of Life, who proceedeth from the Father, who with the Father and the Son together is worshipped and glorified, who spoke by the Prophets;

And we believe in one, holy, catholic and apostolic Church.

We acknowledge one baptism for the remission of sins.

We look for the resurrection of the dead,

And the life of the age to come. Amen.

Not Made With Hands

One of the earliest Icons witnessed to by Church Tradition is the Icon of the Savior Not-Made-By-Hands. According to Tradition, during the time of the earthly ministry of the Savior, Abgar ruled in the Syrian city

---

[1]In church services the creed is recited in the first person singular ("I believe . . ."), but it was originally composed by the fathers of the first and second ecumenical councils in the first person plural ("We believe . . .").—*Ed.*

of Edessa. He was afflicted with leprosy over his whole body. At this time report of the great miracles performed by the Lord extended throughout Syria (Mt 4.24) and as far as Arabia. Although not having seen the Lord, Abgar believed in Him as the Son of God and wrote a letter requesting Him to come and heal him. With this letter he sent to Palestine his court-painter Ananias, entrusting him to paint an image of the Divine Teacher.

Ananias went to Jerusalem and saw the Lord surrounded by people. He was not able to go to Him because of the great throng of people listening to His preaching; so he stood on a huge rock and attempted to produce a painting of the image of the Lord Jesus Christ, unable, however, to succeed. The Savior Himself called him by name and gave for Abgar a beautiful letter in which, having glorified the faith of the ruler, He promised to send His disciple in order to heal him from the leprosy and instruct him in salvation.

After this, the Lord called for water and a towel. He wiped His face, rubbing with the towel, and on it was impressed His Divine Image. The towel and the letter the Savior sent with Ananias to Edessa. With thanksgiving Abgar received the sacred object and received healing, but a small portion, only a trace, remained of the terrible disease on his face until the arrival of the promised Disciple of the Lord.

The Apostle of the 70, Thaddeus, came to them and preached the Gospel, baptizing the believing Abgar and all living in Edessa. Having written on the Image Not-Made-By-Hands the words, Christ-God, everyone trusting in Thee will not be put to shame, Abgar adorned it and placed it in a niche over the city gates.

Excerpt from *These Truths We Hold–The Holy Orthodox Church: Her Life and Teachings.* Compiled and Edited by A Monk of St Tikhon's Monastery. (South Canaan, PA: St Tikhon's Seminary Press, 1986), pp.273–274.

Once Saved, Always Saved

Scripture teaches that it is possible for a believer to fall away through sin or unbelief and forfeit his salvation. St Paul warns: "Let him who thinks he stands take care lest he fall" (1 Cor 10.12). He uses the example of the Israelites who passed through the Red Sea with Moses, and yet later fell away and were punished, as a warning to Christians. The Book of Hebrews uses the same example and warns, "Take heed, brethren, lest there be in any one of you an evil heart of unbelief, departing from the living God" (Heb. 3.12). Our eternal salvation depends on our perseverance in Christ: "For we are made partakers of Christ, if we hold the beginning of our confidence steadfast to the end" (Heb. 3.14).

[St Peter writes:] "For if after they have escaped the pollutions of the world though the knowledge of the Lord and Savior Jesus Christ, they are again entangled therein, and overcome, the latter end is worse with them than the beginning. For it would have been better for them not to have known the way of righteousness, than, after they have known it, to turn from the holy commandment delivered unto them" (2 Pet.2.20–1). Clearly, then, it is possible to know Christ and then fall away. The only insurance against it is continuing, daily trust in Christ and struggle against sin. Let us remember the words of Jesus: "Not every one who says to me Lord, Lord, will enter the kingdom of heaven, but he that does the will of my Father who is in heaven" (Mt 7.21). We must, as Peter says, "Strive to make our calling and election sure" (2 Pet 1.10).

> Taken from the pamphlet, "An Eastern Orthodox Response to
> Evangelical Claims", Fr Paul O'Callaghan
> (Minneapolis: Light and Life, 1984), pp. 25–26.

Original Sin & Guilt

It goes without saying that the doctrines of original sin, atonement, and predestination were never understood by Orthodox Christians in an Augustinian, Anselmian, and Calvinistic manner. Original sin is not an inherited guilt, nor is death a punishment from God for such guilt. God permitted death in order that sin might not become eternal. Salvation is not a question of satisfying a wrathful God. God really loves those who refuse to return his love and so are eternally damned. Therefore, anyone who thinks that he has a special claim on the love of God because of any special church affiliation or predestination will be in for a real surprise. On the other hand, he who has confidence in the love of God and is indifferent to the question of salvation will also be in for a surprise.

John S. Romanides—*http://www.romanity.org/htm/rom.07.en.remarks_ of_an_orthodox_christian_on_religious_fre.htm* (accessed August 11, 2017)

For more on the Orthodox understanding of Original Sin & Guilt see: *The Ancestral Sin*, John S. Romanides (Ridgewood, NJ: Zephyr, 1998).

Scholasticism

As now understood, [is] a method of philosophical and theological speculation which aims at a better understanding of revealed truths, that is, as an attempt by intellectual processes, by analogy and by defining, coordinating, and systematizing the data of faith, to attain to a deeper penetration into the inner meaning of Christian doctrine.

ODCC, p.1245.

The Vincentian Canon, 454 A.D

Now in the Catholic Church itself we take the greatest care to hold *that which has been believed everywhere, always and by all.* That is truly and properly 'Catholic,' as is shown by the very force and meaning of the word, which comprehends everything almost universally. We shall hold to this rule if we follow universality [i.e. oecumenicity], antiquity, and consent. We shall follow universality if we acknowledge that one faith to be true which the whole Church throughout the world confesses; antiquity if we in no wise depart from those interpretations which it is clear that our ancestors and fathers proclaimed; consent, if in antiquity itself we keep following the definitions and opinions of all, or certainly nearly all, bishops and doctors alike.

Documents of the Christian Church, Henry Bettenson and Chris Maunder, eds. (Oxford: Oxford University Press, 2011), pp. 89–90.

The Western Rite

A Western Rite parish is to be distinguished from the more usual Eastern or Byzantine Rite parishes. When the Latin Church in the west separated itself from the unity of the Orthodox Church, the venerable and ancient Western liturgy was lost to the Church. In the Nineteenth Century, when the Papal claims of supremacy culminated in the novel doctrine of papal infallibility, the Orthodox Church was approached by Westerners seeking the apostolic purity of the ancient, unchanging Orthodox faith wherein the Bishop of Rome would be considered to have primacy of honor. They would utilize their own familiar and theologically Orthodox liturgical forms, while coincidentally restoring the Western liturgy to the Orthodox Church.

The Holy Synod of Moscow responded by approving the restored form of the Western Liturgy, the ancient Liturgy of St. Gregory the Great. This is the oldest Orthodox liturgy of the undivided Church still in use. The balance was struck involving the Eastern and Western traditions of Orthodoxy. In the twentieth century, the Patriarch of Antioch established the Western Rite Vicariate for North America. The Orthodox Church reclaimed what was rightfully hers.

http://www.antiochian.org/node/22395 (accessed August 11, 2017)

Women's Ordination

My beliefs regarding the question of the ordination of women are based on Scripture, Tradition, the Incarnation and godly women. I've been found in church nearly all my life, thanks to godly women. Years ago, C. S. Lewis had this to say regarding the issue:

> Suppose the reformer stops saying that a good woman is like God and beings saying that God is like a good woman. Suppose he says that we might just as well pray to "Our Mother who art in Heaven" as to "Our Father". Suppose he suggests that the Incarnation might just as well have taken a female as a male form, and the Second Person of the Trinity be as well called the Daughter as the Son. Suppose, finally, that the

mystical marriage were reversed, that the Church is the Bridegroom and Christ the Bride. All this, as it seems to me, is involved in the claim that a woman can represent God as a priest does. Now it is surely the case that if all these supposals were ever carried into effect we should have embarked on a different religion.

C.S. Lewis, "Priestesses in the Church?" in *God in the Dock: Essays on Theology and Ethics*, ed. Walter Hooper (Grand Rapids: William B. Eerdmans, 1970; reprinted, 1982), pp. 236–237.